MW01227313

NCGR
Education Curriculum and Study Guide for Certification Testing

Written and compiled by
The 2003 NCGR Board of Examiners
under the direction
of
Bruce Scofield

National Council for Geocosmic Research, Inc.

ISBN: 0-9648415-1-7

Current Edition Printed: 2003

Production: Kris Brandt Riske
Production assistance: Shirley Soffer, Maria Kay Simms
Cover Design: Jill Thorman

Published by:
National Council for Geocosmic Research
8810-C Jamacha Blvd., PMB 183
Spring Valley CA 91977-5633

Printed in the United States of America

*The NCGR Curriculum is the child of a
national education conference held at
Princeton University in August 1979.
Teachers representing most major astrological disciplines
devised a four-year study program encompassing
modern and traditional concepts.*

Contents

Foreword
A History of NCGR's Education Program

NCGR's Education and Certification Program, recognized internationally for its rigor and excellence, is our most cherished achievement in fulfillment of the Statement of Purpose[1] of our Founders, which includes several specific charges for fulfillment of that purpose. The two most pertinent are:

- *The formulation of a curriculum and the essentials of a course of studies leading to recognized competency in the field of geocosmic studies.*

- *Certification of students and researchers to various levels of competency in geocosmic studies.*

With the publication of this new 2003 *Education Curriculum Study Guide for Certification Testing*, NCGR continues a developmental process begun more than a quarter of a century ago.

Following several years of preliminary planning and work within NCGR Board, under the direction of successive Education Directors Kenneth Negus, Ph.D., Lenore Canter and Sonny Delmonico, with soon-to-be Co-Directors, Joan Negus and Joanna Shannon, a historic national education conference was held at Princeton University in August of 1979. About 50 professional astrologers and teachers of astrology from throughout the United States, including delegates from NCGR's Chapters, gathered for a five day meeting for the specific purpose of creating and launching an educational program. After the framework of the curriculum was established at this meeting, a geographically dispersed committee made up of those delegates whose background included credentials as professional educators worked for a time to refine the program and as a result, a first syllabus was published in

---

1. The full Statement of Purpose appears in the NCGR Constitution and By-Laws. See http://geocosmic.org/about/#purpose

1980. Finally, a smaller National Education Committee of 8-10 members who could meet together regularly in New York with the Co-Directors was entrusted with the task of further development of the curriculum from the initial work, writing a Study Guide, refining and testing the tests, and setting up procedures for giving examinations. This group included Joan and Joanna, Ken Negus, Julian Armistead, Lenore Canter, Helen Huber, Bruce Scofield and Maria Kay Simms (then known as Maria Jossick).

NCGR's program was structured in four successive levels because it was envisioned that someday astrology might be once again studied in colleges and universities, so it would make sense to consider which portions of astrological technique might be studied during each of the four years of typical college training. From the outset it was envisioned that within a major in astrology, the student would also take courses that would support his or her intended specialty, such as psychology for consultants, business and finance, methods in education, history and/or statistics.

Though the focus was on technique, the Education Committee members were well aware that most astrologers do some consulting regardless of whether they have had any formal training in that area, and it may be many years before the vision of astrology within collegiate programs with appropriate supplementary course work could be realized. Because of that, it was decided that the acquiring of counseling skills would be recommended and that at each of the four levels of testing, questions would be

included that required knowledge of and sensitivity to ethics in counseling.

Testing began slowly in 1981, and with the evaluation of results, further refinements were made in methodology. Curriculum Guides for Levels I and II were first published in the "Phoenix" revival issue of *NCGR Journal* in the summer of 1984, and the guide for Levels III and IV was published in the following issue of the Journal. Later, the entire 4-level guide was published as a separate booklet.

Members of the Education Committee felt strongly that no one among them should be given the NCGR certification without testing, because exceptions to the necessity of fulfilling requirements would lessen respect for the program. Because we had tested each other numerous times in the process of writing questions for the first two level tests (for which all questions were objective or calculation exercises), it was decided that we had effectively tested on those levels, but everyone, without exception, would need to take the Level III and IV exams, mostly made up of essay questions and papers to write, and have them juried by others. Since committee members who had previously taken the AFA professional exam were familiar with its requirements as more than adequately covering NCGR's requirements for Levels I and II, it was further decided that proof of having the PMAFA certificate would entitle an applicant to enter testing at Level III.

In 1996, an Education Conference was held in Orlando, Florida with NCGR's first gala Graduation Ceremony, complete with graduation caps. Twenty-seven people who had completed Level IV were awarded their certificates and a special pin.

All too soon after that, NCGR was deeply saddened by the passing of both Joan Negus (1997) and Joanna Shannon (1998). Helen Huber and Bruce Scofield became the new Co-Directors. They formed a Board of Examiners to assist them in administering the testing program, and continuing the development of the curriculum.

In 1999, in response to requests to allow some kind of qualifying for comparable work, and in recognition of the fact that our program was in need of momentum, a one-year window of time was allowed when applicants could qualify to enter at Level IV by presenting proof of equivalency. The program was launched with an announcement of criteria in *Memberletter*, and was conducted rigorously, with each applicant receiving a list of documents to be gathered and requirements to meet, depending on which Level IV certification track he or she wished to pursue. A member of the Board of Examiners, who then wrote an evaluation, juried each applicant's documents and papers. Not all who applied passed and the program closed as scheduled, at the end of 1999.

As of this publication there are 1468 members of NCGR who have participated in our Education Program and have been certified in one or more levels. There are 111 who have become Level IV certified in one or more of our four tracks. Those who have achieved Level IV are authorized to put the initials C.A.

NCGR after their names.

NCGR is a firm supporter of Kepler College of Astrological Arts and Sciences of Seattle, the first college to be authorized by its state to grant bachelor's and master's degrees in astrology. We are most gratified that NCGR's program, testing through Level III, has been approved for challenge of credit in Kepler's courses in astrological technique. Also, with NCGR Level III plus a bachelor's degree from an accredited college or university, one can apply directly to Kepler's master's degree program.

Since our program's approval by Kepler, NCGR has also explored reciprocal accreditation with a few other programs, whose curricula are closely equivalent to ours. We recognize that NCGR members who have proof of completion of clearly equivalent programs should be able to challenge the necessity to take one or more of our lower level exams. Recently we have arrived at such an agreement with Online College of Astrology, whereby those graduates of OCA who have completed appropriate course work in its certification track will be allowed to enter NCGR testing at Level IV. We are currently working toward a reciprocal accreditation agreement with Canadian Association for Astrological Education. It has been decided on the recommendation of our Co-Education Directors and approved by NCGR Board, that our granting of qualifying credit to an applicant for our testing can, in no case, be applied beyond Level III. All applicants for the C.A. (Certified Astrologer) NCGR must complete the requirements for one of our Level IV tracks.

In recent years, in recognition of the need to refine and update our curriculum, and to add material on the ancient/classical techniques that have been revived through the work of Project Hindsight and Arhat, plus the increasingly popular Vedic astrology, the Board of Examiners, under the direction of Bruce Scofield, has worked diligently to prepare this revised and updated study guide, plus the first set of new examinations. Members of the Board of Examiners, then, as authors of this Guide include:

David Arner
Helen Huber
Terry Lamb
Kenneth Negus, Ph.D.
Joseph Polis
Bruce Scofield
Kaye Shinker
Jackie Slevin
Shirley Soffer
Ena Stanley

We also gratefully acknowledge the work of Madela Ezcura, who serves on our Board of Examiners as Spanish translator, since our exams are available and can be taken in Spanish. Our thanks also to Joseph Crane for his information and editorial assistance with the material on ancient/classical astrology.

Bruce Scofield stepped down as Co-Director of Education at the end of 2002 in order to focus on a doctoral program and his teaching assignments at Kepler College. Ena Stanley, head of OCA and the first C.A. NCGR to receive her certificate as Professional Instructor, was appointed to replace him.

NCGR's Education Certification Program has withstood the test of time, and continues forward, anticipating future growth and development. With pride and pleasure we present this new 2003 edition of *NCGR Education Curriculum and Study Guide for Certification Testing*.

Maria Kay Simms, C.A. NCGR, Chair

NCGR Curriculum

The NCGR education program is designed to give structure to astrological studies in order to raise the standards of the field for both students and teachers. It is designed to be used as a major in a four-year college curriculum. Additional educational opportunities are offered through approved schools, national conferences, master classes, and selected chapter programs.

Level I

Level I provides the building blocks in the foundation of Western astrology. In order to pass a proficiency examination at this level the student must comprehend the signs, planets, houses, personal points (Ascendant, MC, Moon's Nodes), major aspects and their configurations; and be able to apply them in natal interpretation. Some knowledge of the basics of classical (inspired by ancient and medieval) astrology is also required at this level. In addition the student learns to calculate a natal chart for any geographical location. Astronomy is studied on each level, becoming increasingly more detailed as the student progresses. The topics introduced on Level I include the solar system, eclipses, retrograde motion, and solstices. These are developed in greater depth at the higher levels.

Level II

On Level II, natal delineation is reviewed and minor aspects, lunar phases, derived houses, asteroids and fixed stars are added to broaden interpretation. The dynamic elements of astrology (which include transits, progressions, and solar arcs) are also introduced at this level. Additional elements of classical astrology are covered. Various systems of house division are compared. Calculations include relocation charts, transits, progressions, solar arc directions, declinations, the Vertex, the Equatorial Ascendant, and antiscia (solstice points). Acquaintance with mundane charting such as ingress charts is required at this level, but is covered more fully in Level III.

Level III

Level III introduces the 360° and 90° dials for more precision and covers the subjects of horary and electional astrology, synastry, composites, solar and lunar returns, and the history of astrology. A survey level familiarity with other astrological disciplines is expected: specifically Uranian, etc. A take-home test on mundane astrology is also required at this level.

Level IV

Level IV solidifies the information of the other levels and adds rectification (which can incorporate many techniques). Once rectification is passed the student may specialize in consulting, technical research, instruction, or general research.

For more information about
NCGR's Education Curriculum
and Certification Testing, contact:

Jackie Slevin
P.O. Box 8253
Glen Ridge NJ 07028

Ena Stanley
P.O. Box 85
Basye VA 22810

www.geocosmic.org

edu@geocosmic.org

Study Guide for Level I

Introduction

Introduction to Astrology

Dictionaries define astrology as a study that attempts to understand the affairs of human beings by studying the stars and planets. In essence, astrology is exactly that — but it is also more. Astrologers read character and destiny from a map of the sky computed for the time and place of birth, a map called the horoscope. The positions of the planets in the horoscope symbolize a person's basic character, prominent personality traits, and also provide the timing of major life events. A good astrologer is also able to deduce something about a person's spouse, parents, children, and even pets from that person's horoscope.

Ptolemy (c. 150 AD), the greatest scientist of the ancient world and author of the major astrological work, the *Tetrabiblos*, divided astrology into two fundamental categories: *universal* and *genethlialogical*. The former was concerned with natural phenomena such as climate, weather, earthquakes, agriculture, plagues, etc. The later was con-

cerned with the affairs of individuals. By the Renaissance these two branches were known as *natural* and *judicial* astrology respectively. Many of the founders of modern science either practiced natural astrology or had no quarrel with it. In modern times this branch has also been called *mundane* astrology and its area of inquiry was extended to history, politics, and the fates of nations. Judicial astrology was and is far more controversial. Traditionally, this branch included *natal* astrology, *horary* astrology, and *electional* astrology, all of which deal with the life patterns of humans. In modern times, the astrology of individuals is called natal astrology, and horary and electional is called judicial astrology.

A real understanding of astrology begins with the concept that it is basically a system, code, or language that uses symbols: the Sun, Moon and planets, zodiac signs, houses, and aspects. These symbols correspond to very specific categories of things, events, arenas of life, and personality traits. An astrologer blends combinations of these symbols and makes deductions about a person or situation. This act of interpretation is gleaned from a long tradition of knowledge and experience. Familiarity with astronomy is also necessary in order to create the schematic map of the sky commonly called the horoscope. Astrologers use astronomical data, mathematics, and computers to determine precisely how the sky was or will be configured at a given place and time.

Although astrology is very different from the hard sciences like physics or chemistry, it is a technical study in itself. Natural astrology, for example, investigates linkages between physical phenomena and planetary cycles. Of the other sciences, astrology can best be compared to medicine or psychology, both of which use technical knowledge along with personal judgment calls. Astrology, like medicine and psychology, applies its methodology to the human condition. Consulting astrology, in particular, is a diagnostic art that makes use of technical data.

Where astrology differs radically from conventional Western science is its use of a different kind of logic, one that assumes that things are interconnected. Conventional Western science is concerned with separations and boundaries that can be measured exactly. Astrology is holistic and works with correlations and linkages. Science seeks control over nature while astrology seeks to harmonize with nature. In a very real sense, astrology is concerned with the ecology of body, mind, and spirit on this planet. There are, however, newer emerging branches of science that may turn out to be more receptive to astrology.

Astrology has generally retained its continuity with an earlier time when humankind was not separate from nature. Modern astrology is based on more than 4,000 years of observations that have been constantly revised and updated. Just as ancient medicine is not the medicine practiced today, ancient Mesopotamian or Renaissance astrology is not the astrology of contemporary times. Much has been added to the astrological paradigm through other disciplines aside from astrology, such as geology, psychology, and ecology. Nevertheless, astrology continues to prove its value today, as it did in ancient times.

Ethics

Beginning students should mainly concentrate on learning the principles of astrology and applying these to general interpretation. Although one learns by interpreting charts for family and friends, the beginner must be cautious, and should avoid discussing critical or sensitive issues, unless he or she has had substantial prior training in counseling techniques. Avoid making any type of predictive statements at this Level, and take care to avoid any interpretive comment that may be psychologically damaging.

Keep in mind that there are always multiple things that can be said, interpretively, about any factor in astrology. Put yourself in the other's place. Often HOW something is said is much more important than WHAT is said, in terms of how it is HEARD by the other. When you point out multiple options for how a factor in someone's chart might be interpreted and listen carefully to his/her feedback, you empower that person's personal ability and responsibility to choose, and open yourself to greater learning..

It is highly recommended that anyone who aspires to be an astrological consultant read and take seminars and courses in counseling techniques. Also read carefully the NCGR Code of Ethics, to which all NCGR members, in accordance with our by-laws, are accountable.

Planets

Planets represent functions, agents, energies and life principles.

Glyphs

⊙ Sun
☽ Moon
☿ Mercury
♀ Venus
♂ Mars
♃ Jupiter
♄ Saturn
♅ Uranus
♆ Neptune
♇ Pluto

⊙ *life energy*
⊙ *sense of SELF/ego*

Keywords *need to individuate*

Sun—vitality, ego, will, individuality, father, purpose, being, authority, creativity, pride, self-image

Moon—emotions, feelings, response, mother, women, (public,) memory, nurturance, changeability *, unconscious*

Mercury—communication, logic, reason, dexterity, speech, writing, wit, cleverness

Venus—love, affection, artistry, harmony, beauty, values, attraction, relating, peace, music

Mars—initiative, aggressiveness, courage, desire, energy, passion, will, impulsiveness, force, action, drive

Jupiter—expansiveness, optimism, law, religion, higher education, long journeys, justice, prosperity, generosity, extravagance, excess

Saturn—ambition, responsibility, discipline, limitation, restriction, structure, caution, old age, control, father, delay, inhibition, fear

Uranus—sudden change, rebellion, technology, independence, originality, eccentricity, liberation

Neptune—sensitivity, spirituality, illusion, music, imagination, idealism, deception, dreams, sacrifice, escapism, vagueness, confusion, dancing, film

Pluto—transformation, regeneration, elimination, destruction, compulsion, death, power, deep analysis

Dignities and Debilities

Traditionally the qualities of planets are considered more easily (or less easily) expressed in certain signs than in others.

Categories include:

Rulership—Planets are considered strongest in the signs they rule

Exaltation—Second strongest placement of a planet

Dignities and Debilities

Sign	Ruler	Detriment	Exaltation	Fall
Aries	Mars	Venus	Sun	Saturn
Taurus	Venus	Mars	Moon	Uranus
Gemini	Mercury	Jupiter	North Node	South Node
Cancer	Moon	Saturn	Neptune	Mars
Leo	Sun	Uranus	---	Mercury (Modern)
Virgo	Mercury	Neptune	Mercury	Venus (Ancient)
Libra	Venus	Mars	Saturn	Sun
Scorpio	Mars (Ancient Pluto (Modern)	Venus	Uranus	Moon
Sagittarius	Jupiter	Mercury	South Node	North Node
Capricorn	Saturn	Moon	Mars	Neptune
Aquarius	Saturn/ (Ancient) Uranus (Modern)	Sun	Mercury	---
Pisces	Jupiter (Ancient Neptune (Modern)	Mercury	Venus	Mercury

Detriment (found in the sign opposite its rulership)—Considered a weak placement for the planet

Fall (found in the sign opposite its exaltation)—Considered the weakest placement for the planet

Note: Astrologers who practice classical astrology do not use the modern planets — Uranus, Neptune, and Pluto—in categories of ruler, detriment, exaltation, or fall.

Benefics/Malefics

According to classical astrology, there are many ways of determining planetary strength. The following are the most general: Venus and Jupiter are considered benefic or fortunate planets; Mars and Saturn malefics or unfortunate planets. Other planets are considered neutral.

Planetary Sect

Planetary sect divides the planets into the diurnal and nocturnal.

The diurnal planets are Sun, Jupiter, and Saturn; the nocturnal planets are Moon, Venus, and Mars. Mercury is diurnal if it rises before the Sun, nocturnal if it sets after the Sun. In a diurnal birthchart (Sun above the horizon), the diurnal planets have some advantage; in a nocturnal birthchart (Sun below the horizon), the nocturnal planets have some advantage.

Also, diurnal planets prefer to be on the same side of the horizon as the Sun and in masculine (fire or air) signs; nocturnal planets prefer to be on the other side of the horizon as the Sun and in feminine (earth or water) signs.

Mutual Reception

Planetary strength may be <u>enhanced</u> through mutual reception, whereby two planets are in each others' signs of dignity and thus are in a position to help each other. This is especially the case if the two planets are in signs that aspect each other, or if a planet is dignified. For example: Sun in Aries and Mars in Leo (signs are in trine relationship; also Sun is in its exaltation). If one or both planets are also debilitated, such as Mercury in Sagittarius and Jupiter in Gemini, the benefits of mutual reception hardly obtain.

In classical astrology, a mutual reception could also happen between Planet A in the sign ruled by Planet B and Planet B in the sign in which Planet A is exalted; or between two planets in exaltation signs of the other. Examples are: Venus in Aries and Mars in Pisces; or Moon in Aries and Sun in Cancer; or Moon in Libra and Saturn in Taurus.

Retrogrades

The qualities of retrograde planets are internalized, reversed, or slower to develop.

The Sun and Moon are never retrograde.

For illustration of retrograde motion see Diagram 6 in this study guide.

Signs

Signs represent characteristics and describe *how* a planet's energies are expressed

Qualities

Polarities
Active signs (positive) (+) are masculine, yang, initiating, extroverted

Receptive signs (negative) (-) are feminine, yin, responding, introverted

Modes (quadruplicities)
Cardinal—initiative and direct approach

Fixed—persistence and goal orientation

Mutable—fluctuation, adaptability and social interaction

Elements (triplicities)
Fire—enthusiasm, zeal, warmth, idealism, creativity

Earth—practicality, materialism, realism, concreteness

Air—mental activity, abstraction, communication, objectivity

Water—emotions, intuition, compassion, subjectivity

Glyphs

♈—Aries
♉—Taurus
♊—Gemini
♋—Cancer
♌—Leo
♍—Virgo
♎—Libra
♏—Scorpio
♐—Sagittarius
♑—Capricorn
♒—Aquarius
♓—Pisces

Keywords

Aries—active, spontaneous, initiating, self-assertive, energetic, naive, "me first," ardent, leader

Taurus—stable, persistent, sensual, materialistic, possessive, security-oriented, comfort-loving, patient, determined, stubborn, practical

Gemini—restless, communicative, curious, versatile, flexible, quick-witted, diversified, scattered

Cancer¾sensitive, emotional, instinctual, sentimental, memory-retentive, nurturing, self-protective, family/mother/home-oriented

Leo—warm-hearted, loyal, generous, dramatic, proud, regal, creative, dominating

Virgo—discriminating, service-oriented, pro-ductive, health-conscious, analytical, critical

Libra—cooperative, partnership-oriented, social, appreciative of beauty, fair, balancing, indecisive, indolent

Scorpio—intense, penetrating, secretive, jealous, introspective, passionate, strong-willed, possessive; urge for intimacy; death and regeneration

Sagittarius—optimistic, enthusiastic, candid, adventurous, truth-seeking, philosophical, judgmental, tactless

Capricorn—responsible, ambitious, managerial, reserved, dutiful, cautious, somber, status-seeking

Aquarius—detached, humanitarian, individualistic, non-conforming, independent, aloof, impersonal

Pisces—imaginative, self-sacrificing, impressionable, sympathetic, compassionate, illusionary, secretive, victimizing or victimized

Planetary rulerships of signs are given above in the section on dignities and debilities.

Houses

Houses represent areas or departments of life; categories or issues

Keywords

First house—physical body, personality, beginnings, personal appearance

Second house—personal values, material resources or possessions, physical senses, self-worth, talent, earning capacity

Third house—communications, early education, conscious mind, siblings, everyday ideas, neighbors and neighborhood, short trips

Fourth house—home, comfort, security, ancestry, real estate, foundations, family affairs, domestic parent

Fifth house—children, creative self-expression, speculation, sports, entertainment, love affairs, hobbies, pleasure-sharing friends

Sixth house—service, physical health, co-workers, daily work or routine, small animals

Seventh house—signficant partnerships (marriage or business), psychotherapy, lawsuits, known opponents, one-to-one relationships

Eighth house—death and regeneration, psychoanalysis, inheritance, taxes, surgery, other people's resources, corporate finances, banking, debts

Ninth house—philosophy, religion, higher education, law, distant travel

Tenth house—social status, reputation, profession, career, employer, outer-world parent, life-direction

Eleventh house—like-minded friends, networks and groups, organizations, shared hopes, wishes, dreams, contacts

Twelfth house—unconscious mind, institutions, confinement, secrets, sanctuaries, self-undoing, activities behind the scenes, secret enemies, large animals

Quadrants

First quadrant (houses 1, 2 and 3)—the quadrant of self-development

Second quadrant (houses 4, 5 and 6)—the quadrant of self-expression

Third quadrant (houses 7, 8 and 9)—the quadrant of awareness of others

Fourth quadrant (houses 10, 11 and 12)—the quadrant of world consciousness

Angularity

The angular houses are 1, 4, 7 and 10:

- First house—I am
- Fourth house—I feel
- Seventh house—I relate
- Tenth house—I use

The succedent houses are 2, 5, 8, and 11:

- Second house—I have
- Fifth house—I will
- Eighth house—I desire
- Eleventh house—I know

The cadent houses are 3, 6, 9 and 12:

- Third house—I think
- Sixth house—I analyze
- Ninth house—I comprehend
- Twelfth house—I believe

Interception

Occurs in certain house systems (e.g., Placidus) and more often at higher latitudes.

With interception, one whole sign and parts of two others are in the same house. An intercepted sign never appears on the cusp of a house. If one sign is intercepted, its oppositional sign is also intercepted.

Derivation

The houses can also symbolize persons in the native's life derived by a special counting technique. For example, because the 7th house symbolizes the partner, the 8th house would represent the partner's 2nd house, and, therefore, can be used to investigate the partner's resources.

Personal Points (in addition to Sun and Moon)

Ascendant—personality, physical appearance, birth, self-perception

Midheaven—career, profession, honor, prestige, perception by others

Moon's Nodes—relationships, connections, contacts, talents and/or obsessions

Aspects

Definition: the angular relationship between two points, expressed in degrees. Some aspects are considered more powerful than others and have various qualities.

Orbs

An orb is the arc (in degrees) within which an aspect is judged to be effective. There is some disagreement on the subject, so on tests, orbs to use will be indicated.

Aspects may be "in-sign" (e.g., Mars at 3° Aries trine Venus at 5° Leo). Or aspects may be "out-of-sign" (e.g., Mars at 3° Aries trine Venus at 29° Cancer).

Aspects may be exact, applying or separating.

An aspect is applying when the faster moving planet is at an earlier degree than the slower moving planet.

An aspect is separating when the faster moving planet is at a later degree than the slower moving planet.

Glyphs

☌—Conjunction
⊻—Semisextile
∠—Semisquare
✶—Sextile
□—Square
△—Trine
⊡—Sesquisquare
☍—Opposition

Introduction to Aspects

Conjunction (division of the circle by 1) 0° or 360°—Considered the most powerful aspect because of sign emphasis, but varying in meaning according to the planets involved.

Opposition (division of the circle by 2) 180°—A polarity that shows a need to balance opposing forces. May be separative, or indicate enlightenment and awareness if integrated.

Trine (division of the circle by 3) 120°—A soft aspect, indicating a cooperative energy flow between two points.

Square (division of the circle by 4) 90°—A hard aspect, releasing tremendous energy which needs to be channeled and resolved. May be a building block or a stumbling block.

Sextile (division of the circle by 6) 60°—A soft aspect, offering opportunity or help from others.

Quincunx (five-twelfths of the circle) 150°—Indicates strain and/or adjustment, sometimes related to health.

Semisextile (one-twelfth of the circle) 30°—In the same harmonic sequence as the quincunx, it indicates a minor strain or adjustment.

Semisquare (one-eighth of the circle) 45°—Similar to the square but less powerful.

Sesquiquadrate (three-eights of the circle) 135°—Similar to the semisquare but involves sudden stress.

Major Configurations

Stellium—Three or more planets in the same sign or house. A sign stellium indicates that the sign is strongly emphasized in the character of the native. A house stellium signifies an area of emphasis.

Grand Trine—Three planets 120° apart forming an equilateral triangle. The planets are ideally in the same element (fire, earth, air, or water). Easy flow, or sometimes over-emphasis of the elements and planets involved.

Grand Cross—Two oppositions involving four planets in square to each other, ideally in the same mode (cardinal, fixed or mutable). Combines the definition of the square with the opposition. One of the most stressful configurations, but potentially creative. The individual must learn to mediate the energies to use them effectively.

T-square—Three planets of which two are in opposition and a third, focal planet is square both. Similar quality as the Grand Cross but less stressful, since the outlet for the stress is found in the house opposite the focal planet.

Grand Sextile—Six planets in sextile to each other in six different signs. This configuration does not occur frequently. It indicates emphasis of fire/air or earth/water. It also combines the qualities of the sextile, trine, and opposition. Often indicative of high achievement and dynamism.

Yod (Finger of God)—Two planets in sextile to each other and both quincunx a third, focal planet. Mixed configuration that suggests a radical point of view, often involving a sacrifice.

Interpretation

Hemisphere Emphasis

East (left of the MC-IC axis)—one indication of an initiator

West (right of the MC-IC axis)—one indication of a responder

South (above the Ascendant-Descendant axis)—personal validity through interaction with the world; objective; extroverted energies

North (below the Ascendant-Descendant axis)—personal validity through interaction with the self; subjective; introverted energies

Quadrant emphasis (listed under Houses)

Temperament Patterns or Shapings

Synthesis—Correlation and integration of the basic factors of astrology (planets, personal points, houses, signs, and aspects)

Calculations

Students must be able to calculate house cusps accurately within 1° of arc, and planets within 5' of arc. Students should also be able to erect charts for both east and west longitudes, north and south latitudes.

Calculation Tools and References

- Ephemerides
- Tables of houses
- Time changes books
- Longitude and Latitude books

Accurate Birth Data

The importance of obtaining accurate birth data should be emphasized.

U.S. Government publication Where to Write for Vital Records, DHHS Publication No. (PHS) (Note: need to insert last two digits of current year)-1142. May be purchased through the Superintendent of Documents, US Government Printing Office, Washington, DC 20402

Explanation of Time

- Sidereal Time
- Clock Time (Standard and Daylight Savings Time)
- Conversion of Longitude to Time
- Local Mean Time

Acceptable Methods of Calculating Houses

- Direct
- Employing Local Mean Time
- Four-function Calculator
- Trigonometry
- Logarithms
- Sexagesimal Calculator

Planetary Corrections

- Four-function Calculator
- Logarithms
- Tables of Diurnal Motion

Astronomical Information

The Solar System

The solar system consists of the central sun and nine large bodies or planets revolving around it. The elliptical path each planet follows around the sun is called an orbit. These nine planets, in order of distance from the sun are: Mercury, Venus, Earth, Mars, Jupiter, Saturn, Uranus, Neptune and Pluto. Most of these planets have one or more satellites revolving around them. The moon is Earth's only natural satellite.

See Diagram 1 in this study guide for an illustrated view of the solar system.

Also contained within the solar system are thousands of smaller bodies called asteroids and planetoids, most of which are found between the orbits of Mars and Jupiter.

The View from Earth

Although the sun is the center of the solar system, we live on Earth and see the universe as revolving around us. This is known as an Earth-centered or geocentric view. From our viewpoint on Earth, the sun seems to travel around us once a day and through a circular background of stars once a year. In reality, this apparent motion of the sun is due to certain motions of our own planet. One motion is called rotation which is simply Earth spinning around a central axis, much like a toy top does. One complete turn takes approximately 24 hours or one day. The other motion is called revolution, the movement of Earth around the sun. It takes approximately 365 days or one year for one complete revolution.

24 hrs rotatⁿ vs. revolutⁿ 365 d

The apparent path of the sun against the background of stars is called the ecliptic. All other planets as well as the moon move along this same path, although not exactly on it. Therefore, a band extending 8° on either side of the ecliptic is used

8° band of ecliptic

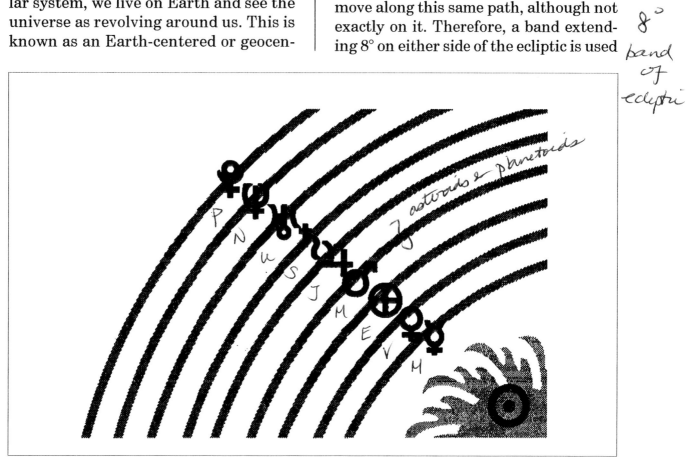

DIAGRAM 1: The Solar System

to include all of the other bodies of the solar system. This band is called the zodiac.

For easy identification, the zodiac was divided into 12 equal segments, each of which was named for the most prominent star group or constellation formerly seen within or approximately within that segment. These sections became known as the signs of the tropical zodiac. At one time the signs corresponded to the constellations for which they were named. Today, however, due to a process called precession of the equinoxes, the correspondence between the tropical sign and the constellation of the same name no longer exists. For example, today we find the constellation of Cancer in the section of the tropical zodiac called Leo.

The Seasons

Earth's axis is not straight up and down in relation to its orbit around the sun. If we could stand out in space at a 90° angle to Earth's orbit, we would see that Earth tilts by about 23°. This tilt is responsible for the seasons. It is also responsible for the difference in the length of daylight during the seasons. See Diagram 2 in this study guide illustrating Earth's annual journey around the sun.

Solstices

The solstices occur when the sun reaches its maximum distance (23°27') north or south of the equator. The vernal and autumnal equinoxes occur when the sun crosses the celestial equator. At the summer solstice the sun has reached its maximum distance above the celestial equa-

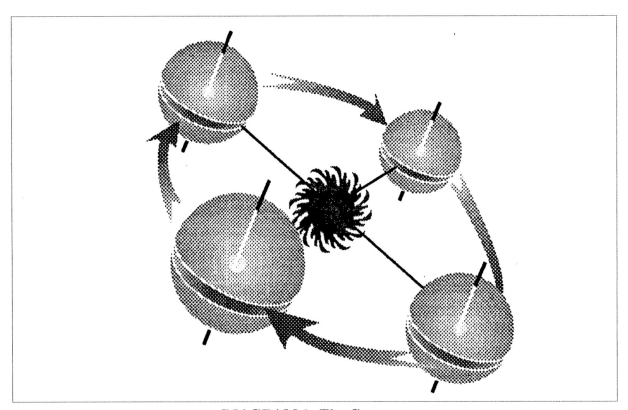

DIAGRAM 2: The Seasons

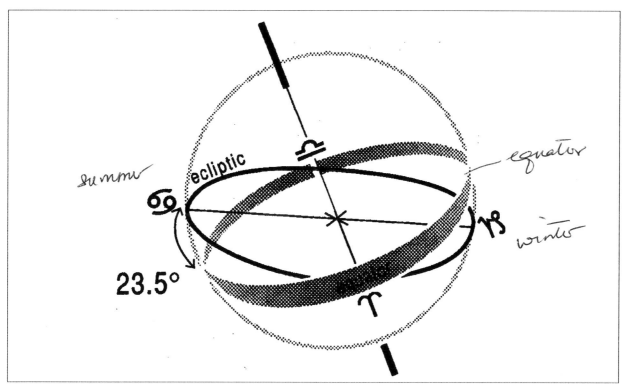

DIAGRAM 3: The Solstices

tor, and at the winter solstice the sun has reached its maximum distance below the celestial equator. In the northern hemisphere these solstices correspond with the seasons; but in the southern hemisphere, summer begins with the winter solstice. This is due to the fact that these concepts were developed in the northern hemisphere.

The vernal equinox correlates with the sun at 0° Aries and the autumnal equinox with the sun at 0° Libra. The sun reaches its maximum distance north of the equator when it is at 0° Cancer. This is the summer solstice. And when the sun reaches its greatest distance south of the equator at 0° Capricorn it is the winter solstice. See Diagram 3 in this study guide for an illustration of the solstices.

Eclipses

There are two kinds of eclipses, solar and lunar.

A solar eclipse occurs at the new moon when the moon passes between the sun and Earth, casting a shadow on Earth.

A lunar eclipse occurs at the full moon, when Earth is between the sun and the moon, and the shadow of Earth falls on the moon. See Diagrams 4 and 5 in this study guide for illustrations of eclipses.

Retrograde Motion

All the planets revolve around the sun from west to east. This is called direct motion. However, since Earth is in motion at the same time, and each of the planets travels at a different speed, they

DIAGRAMS 4 & 5: Eclipses (above, solar eclipse; below, lunar eclipse)

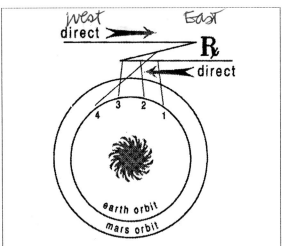

DIAGRAM 6: Retrograde Motion

sometimes appear to gradually slow down, stop, and begin to move in a reverse or backward direction. When a planet appears to move in this reverse direction it is said to be retrograde. When a planet appears to be motionless, it is at its station and is said to be stationary. See Diagram 6 in this study guide illustrating retrograde motion.

An analogous situation would be two trains traveling in the same direction at slightly different speeds. As the faster train overtakes the slower, passengers in it would see the slower train initially moving forward. And when both trains are side by side, the slower one will appear to slow down and the illusion that it has come to a halt will occur. As the faster train passes, the slower train appears to move backwards even though it has not stopped its forward motion.

Retrograde motion is a kind of optical illusion caused by the motion of the planets involved. All of the planets appear to be in retrograde motion at one time or another. The sun and the moon are never retrograde.

Study Guide for Level II

Review and Synthesis: Major aspect configurations   Temperament patterns. Refer to Level I Guide for definitions. Understanding of the material, at this level, should progress beyond key word definitions to synthesis of interpretation.

Potential Uses of Chart Interpretation

Character analysis for any entity that is born or created. Timing of events, either cyclic or for forecasting. Answering specific questions—horary astrology.

Ethics

See this section in the Level I Guide and reread it very carefully, along with the NCGR Code of Ethics. As you begin to study forecasting techniques, keep in mind that multiple options very much apply. Empower others in their personal ability and responsibility to choose. In the test for this Level and beyond, questions involving consulting ethics will be included and will stress common sense and a positive, constructive approach.

Different Zodiacal Systems

Tropical

Utilizes a zodiac that is tied to the seasonal cycle, and begins with the vernal equinox that establishes 0° Aries.

Sidereal

Utilizes a zodiac based upon the constellations of fixed stars which coincided with the signs of the tropical zodiac about 2000 years ago. The sidereal zodiac moves backward through the tropical zodiac at the rate of approximately 50 seconds per year or 1 degree every 72 years. This motion is known as precession.

Planets

Mutual Reception

See Level I Guide for review. Two planets in mutual reception are interpreted as working together as a unit.

Dispositor

Ruler of the sign in which another planet is placed. For example, if Mars is in Libra, Venus (ruler of Libra) is said to be the dispositor of Mars. The driving energy of Mars is thus softened by Venus and Libra.

Final Dispositor

In some charts, a chain of dispositors is formed, where one planet is said to be the final dispositor of all other planets in the chart, since all the other planets ultimately disposit to it. To qualify as a final dispositor, a planet (and only one planet) must be in a sign it rules or co-rules. At least one other planet must also be in that same sign. The final dispositor represents especially strong energies in a person's life.

Decanates

Although the 30° span of a sign encompasses a full sign, the decanate theory is that the first 10° of each sign most strongly represent the qualities of that sign. The next 10° of that sign include qualities of the next sign in the same quadruplicity, and the final 10° include qualities of the third sign in that quadruplicity. (For example, the first 10° of Aries represent the qualities of Aries most, the second 10° of Aries include Leonine qualities, and the final

10° of Aries include Sagittarian qualities).

Minor Aspects

All aspects result from the division of the 360° circle by whole numbers. For example, the trine (120°) is obtained by dividing 360° by 3. Minor aspects result from the division of the circle as follows:

- Divisor of 5: Quintile Series (72°, 144°)

- Divisor of 7: Septile Series (51.43°, 103.86°, 155.29°)

- Divisor of 8: Semisquare/Sesquiquadrate (45°, 135°)

- Divisor of 9: Nonile Series (40°, 80°, 160°)

- Divisor of 12: Semisextile/Quincunx (30°, 150°)

- Divisor of 16: Semioctile Series (22.5°,67.5°,112.5°,157.5°)

Derived House Analysis

Particular houses in the natal chart can be used to evaluate situations concerning any number of other people.

Example: To find one's brother's wife's sister. The 3rd house describes the brother. In derived house analysis, it is considered the brother's 1st house; the 9th house would then represent the brother's wife (7th house from the 3rd). The 9th house also then becomes the wife's 1st house. The wife's sister is then the 11th house of the chart (3rd house from the 9th).

Lunar and Planetary Phases Theory

Lunar Phases are the angular distances between the Sun and the faster-moving Moon.

New Moon—0° to 45°—birth, emergence, new beginning, projection of new direction

Crescent—45° to 90°—expansion, struggle, crystallization of ideas or direction

First Quarter—90° to 135°—crisis of action, expression and activation of ideas

Gibbous—135° to 180°—analysis and evaluation, overcoming of obstacles

Full Moon—180° to 225° (or to closing sesquiquadrate)—culmination, fulfillment, perfect realization

Disseminating—225° to 270° (or to closing square)—demonstration and performance, distribution

Last quarter—270° to 315° (or to closing semisquare)—crisis of consciousness

Balsamic—315° to 360° (or closing semisquare to conjunction)—release of the past, preparation for and commitment to the future

Planets have the same phase relationships to each other as in the lunar phases. Substitute the slower moving planet for the Sun, and the faster moving planet for the Moon. For example, Mars at 5° Cancer is in the First Quarter phase to Saturn at 5° Aries. Interpretation is similar to that of lunar phases, i.e., a crisis, or a need to manage action is implied.

Astronomical Data

Review material in Level I Guide.

Planetary Cycles

Approximate lengths of planetary cycles are as follows:

Mercury is never more than 28° from the Sun; Venus is never more than 48° from the Sun.

- Mars—2 years
- Jupiter—12 years
- Saturn—29 years
- Uranus—84 years
- Neptune—165 years
- Pluto—245 years

Mundane Planes (Great Circles)

Great Circle

A great circle is defined as any circle, the plane of which passes through the center of a sphere (a sphere is the three-dimensional equivalent of a circle). A circle is defined as having all of its points equidistant from the center point of a plane, while a sphere has all points equidistant from a center point in a space. The celestial sphere is an imaginary sphere of infinite radius surrounding Earth (the terrestrial sphere) and serving as a screen against which all celestial objects are seen.

A sphere is generated by rotating a circle. Any circle whose rotation is capable of producing a specific sphere, with a specific center and a specific radius, will also have the feature of cutting that sphere in exact proportions.

Rational Horizon

The rational horizon (simply called the horizon) is formed by extending the four compass points (north, east, south, and west) onto the celestial sphere, then creating a circle from those points in space, the plane of which is passed through the center of Earth. The poles of this great circle are the zenith (directly above the observer) and nadir (directly below the observer). This is the astronomical or true horizon, the visible horizon being the boundary between the sky and the physical landscape.

Meridian

The meridian is a great circle passing through the observer's zenith, the south point of the horizon, the south celestial pole, the observer's nadir, the north point of the horizon, the north celestial pole, and back to the zenith. This circle divides Earth equally, east and west.

Prime Vertical

The Prime Vertical is a great circle passing through the observer's zenith, the east point of the horizon, the observer's nadir, the west point of the horizon, and back to the zenith. The prime vertical and the meridian intersect at the zenith and nadir.

Celestial Equator

The celestial equator, measuring 90° from the celestial poles, is the Earth's equator extended into space.

Ecliptic

The ecliptic is a great circle created by the plane of Earth's orbit onto the celestial sphere. A less proper astronomical definition: the sun's apparent path around Earth.

Other Astronomical Terms

Declination

The distance of a stellar body north or south of the celestial equator, measured in degrees, minutes and seconds. Analagous to latitude on the terrestrial sphere.

Celestial Latitude

The distance of a stellar body from the ecliptic in degrees, minutes and seconds as measured along the great circle that passes through the ecliptic poles and the stellar body, and therefore at right angles of the ecliptic.

Celestial Longitude

The distance along the ecliptic in degrees, minutes and seconds from the vernal equinox to the point of intersection with the ecliptic, of a great circle passing through a stellar body and the ecliptic poles. It is measured from the vernal equinox in the direction of the Sun's apparent motion from 0° to 360°.

Right Ascension

The measurement eastward along the celestial equator from 0° Aries. Analagous to longitude on the terrestrial sphere.

Equinox

One of the two points of intersection of the ecliptic and the celestial equator. The vernal equinox is the point of 0° longitude and 0° latitude, where the sun crosses the equator about March 21; the autumnal equinox is the point 180° longitude, where the sun crosses the equator about September 22.

Solstice

One of the two places where the sun assumes its greatest declination, these points being halfway between the equinoxes. The summer solstice is the point on the ecliptic (at longitude 90°) where the sun is at its maximum northern declination (+23°27'); the winter solstice is the point on the ecliptic (at longitude 270°) where the sun is at its maximum southern declination (-23°27').

Cardinal Points

The equinox and solstice points — i.e., 0° Aries, Libra, Cancer, and Capricorn.

Precession

The retrogression of the vernal point along the fixed (i.e., sidereal) ecliptic at the rate of about 50 arc seconds per year, or 1° every 72 years. About 2,160 years must pass to move 30° of celestial longitude; and about 26,000 years must pass to move 360° of celestial longitude.

Lunar Nodes

The degrees of intersection where the plane of the moon's orbit crosses the plane of the ecliptic. The point at which the moon crosses the ecliptic from south to north is called the North Node. The opposite point is called the South Node.

Mean, or *Average Nodes* travel backward in the zodiac at a uniform rate of approximately 3 minutes of arc per day.

True Node positions are based on the fact that the moon's orbital plane wobbles. The True Node position can vary from the Mean Node by up to 1°45'.

Planetary Nodes

Degrees where orbital planes of the planets intersect Earth's orbital plane.

Parallels and Contraparallels

These are aspects of declination. Two bodies are considered to be parallel if they are in the same degree of declination, and both are either north or south of the celestial equator.

Example: Mars at 11°S08' and Jupiter at 11°S08'.

They are contraparallel if they are in opposite declinations.

Example: Mars at 11°N08' and Jupiter at 11°S08'.

Most authorities allow a maximum of a 1° orb of aspect and consider parallels to have a quality similar to that of a conjunction, while contraparallels operate similarly to an opposition.

Vertex and Equatorial Ascendant

Vertex

The intersection of the prime vertical and the ecliptic in the west. Thought by researchers to pertain to matters of fate. The vertex is calculated by first subtracting the latitude of birth from 90° (the result is the co-latitude). Then, using the natal IC as if it were the MC, refer to a table of houses and find the corresponding Ascendant at the co-latitude. This is the vertex.

Equatorial Ascendant

The degree of the zodiac that would be rising if one were born at the equator. It is found by interpolating the Ascendant at 0° of latitude according to the correction of a given MC. Sometimes erroneously called the East Point. The East Point is actually the anti-vertex.

Relocation Charting

When a person moves to a different location the energies change within that person's natal chart. This can be sensed intuitively because he or she will feel better in one place than in another. This energy difference can be evaluated for different locations anywhere in the world according to where the planets fall on the four angles of the chart as well as a host of other factors.

To evaluate the energies of a specific location, a relocated chart can be erected. This is done by recalculating the birthchart, using the new location and the equivalent time of birth based on the new location. The house cusps of the relocated chart will change, but the zodiacal positions of the planets should remain the same.

Mundane Charting

Ingress charts

The entry of any orbital body into a sign is termed an ingress chart. The most commonly used ingress charts are those of the Sun entering the cardinal signs. A chart cast for the moment the Sun enters 0° Aries signifies the beginning of the astrological new year. Mundane astrologers cast the Aries ingress chart for the location of the capital of a country, or for any specific place in which they are interested. The chart is interpreted in order to prognosticate governmental issues, social conditions, weather, etc. for the year. Charts for 0° of the other cardinal signs are also widely used for prognosis of the affairs of each season, or quarter of the year.

Eclipses

A chart is cast for the exact time of a lunar or solar eclipse for a specific location. There is a difference of opinion as to the length of time during which the influence of an eclipse is felt.

Lunations

Charts cast for specified locations for the new Moon are read for prognosis of the trends for the month. Charts cast for the full Moon are read for the culmination of what began at the new Moon, or for the trends of the two-week period until the next new Moon.

Planetary Conjunctions

Frequently studied in terms of world trends and the destinies of nations and of large groups of people. These charts are cast for the time of a major cyclic aspect, such as the Jupiter-Saturn conjunction.

House Divisions

There are a number of ways to divide the sphere into the twelve parts astrologers refer to as houses. There is also a good deal of controversy over which particular system of house division is the best and how much it matters in interpreting a chart. Proponents of a specific system argue that the matter of house division is of great importance; however, the proof that one system is superior to another has never been shown. Nevertheless, most astrologers would agree that defining intermediate houses in some fashion is necessary.

Over the past century, the Placidus system has been the most widely used, but that is due to the fact that the Placidian tables were the easiest and least expensive to acquire. Now, however, Koch tables are just as accessible.

Quadrant Systems

Campanus

The prime vertical is divided into twelve equal arcs by lunes (sections of the sphere) whose poles are the north and south points of the horizon. Where the lunes cut the ecliptic are the house cusps. The arcs comprising the lunes are house semi-circles.

Regiomontanus

The celestial equator is divided into twelve equal segments beginning at the east point. The house cusps are formed by the intersections of the house semi-circles with the ecliptic. Since the equator is not perpendicular to the north point-south point axis of the horizon, the houses are not equal.

Time Systems

Systems based on time are distinguished from the systems based on space. However, all the time-based systems may be represented by space. The two systems involve poles. The principle remains the same: the semi-arc of some major mundane sensitive point is trisected, and that trisection becomes the basis for the house division.

Placidus

The house cusp curves are formed by points each of which trisects its own diurnal or nocturnal semi-arc. Where these complex curves cross the ecliptic determine the cusps given in the Placidian tables of houses.

Koch

The diurnal semi-arc of the MC is trisected. Calling the trisections of the semi-arc X, the MC is then rotated backwards through its diurnal semi-arc. At this point the MC comes to the horizon. Then the MC is rotated X degrees off the horizon. The new Ascendant is the 11th house cusp. Rotating the MC another X degrees brings the 12th house cusp to the Ascendant, another X degrees being the 1st house cusp (the final Ascendant)

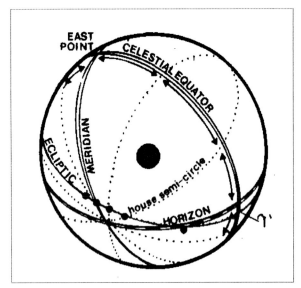

Regiomantanus House System: In Regiomantanus the celestial equator is divided into twelve equal segments beginning at the east point.

to the Ascendant, another X degrees brings the 2nd house cusp to the Ascendant, and finally another X degrees brings the 3rd house cusp to the Ascendant.

Space Systems

Meridian (or equatorial houses). The celestial equator is divided into twelve equal arcs by lunes from the poles of the celestial equator. The intersections of lunes with the ecliptic are considered the house cusps. Each house is exactly two sidereal hours long. The MC is the cusp of the 10th house and the equatorial ascendant is the cusp of the 1st house.

Ancient House Systems

Ancient astrology used the following three house systems, all of which divide the zodiac to create the twelve houses. These three house systems are also used by modern western and vedic astrologers.

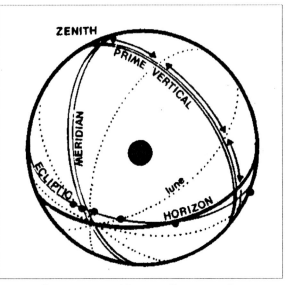

Campanus House System: In Campanus the prime vertical is divided into twelve equal arcs by lunes.

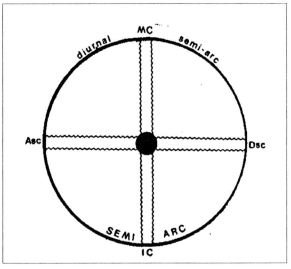

Placidus and Koch House Systems: Placidus trisects all possible semi-arcs. Koch trisects only the diurnal semi-arc of the MC.

Whole Sign

According to the whole sign house method, the 1st house begins at 0° of the sign of the Ascendant, and the remaining houses are signs of the zodiac following the sign of the 1st house. For example, in a chart with 5° Scorpio rising, all of Scorpio is always the 1st house, Aries is the 6th house, and Virgo the 11th house. In this system, neither the Ascendant nor the Midheaven are necessarily house cusps.

Equal House

The equal house system uses the degree of the Ascendant as the 1st house cusp, and the remaining houses are exactly 30° from the Ascendant degree, so that, in the above example of a 5° Scorpio rising, the 6th house cusp is 5° Aries, the 11th house cusp is 5° Virgo. Although the Ascendant is the 1st house cusp, the Midheaven is not necessarily the 10th house cusp.

Porphyry

Porphyry is the first known quadrant system. This method trisects all the quadrants between the four angles of the chart, so that the succedant houses are 1/3rd the distance from angle to angle, and the cadent houses are 2/3rds the distance.

Planetary Rulerships and Disposition

This Table of Essential Dignities gives classical determination of planetary rulership and disposition. The 5-dignity system is a medieval synthesis of different ancient traditions and is used by traditional astrologers in horary as well as natal astrology.

Essential Dignity

Essential dignity shows how much a planet has hegemony due to its placement in the sign and degree of the zodiac.

For example, using Saturn at 3° Libra in a day chart:

- Venus is the sign ruler, Saturn the exaltation, Moon is the face ruler.
- Saturn is the triplicity ruler for a diurnal chart ("D" stands for "day"). Saturn is also the term ruler for the first several degrees of Libra.
- According to tradition, Saturn here would be very highly dignified, even though it is not the sign ruler.

Essential dignity can be quantified by assigning five points to sign ruler, four to exaltation, three to triplicity, two to term, and one to face. Detriment would get minus five, fall minus four, and planets without any essential dignity (peregrine) minus five. Thus, Saturn would get nine points at 3° Libra.

(Note: Some traditional sources, notably William Lilly, have a point system for "accidental dignity," another condition that would make a planet stronger. Accidentally dignified planets may be in the 1st or 10th houses, have trines from Venus or Jupiter, or be swift of motion.)

Disposition

Disposition describes the ruler of the zodiacal place of a planet, Ascendant, or Midheaven.

Almuten

An almuten, meaning overlord or dominator, is the most influential planet in a chart, its strength being determined by its essential and accidential dignities. In the position of 3° Libra in a day chart (see above example), the almuten is Saturn, followed by Venus.

Transits

Transits should be thoroughly studied at Level II. Students should know the length of each planetary cycle (see Planetary Cycles in this study guide). Special emphasis should be placed on the timing and meaning of hard aspects (conjunctions, squares and oppositions) made by outer planets (Jupiter through Pluto) to their natal positions.

Testing will likely include questions about simple interpretation of transit effects, transits as triggers, and generational themes of outer planet transits.

Students should also familiarize themselves with transit tracking (i.e., following transits in the ephemeris).

Secondary Progressions

One day of actual planetary motion in the ephemeris is symbolically representative of one year in a person's life.

ACD (Adjusted Calculation Date, or Limiting Date)

The ACD is the starting date during the year on which the secondary progressions begin. It is the day on which the planetary positions in the ephemeris are accurate as given, without any interpolation. Level II testing requires the calculation of secondary progressions according to the ACD method.

Table of Essential Dignities

Sg.	Domi.	Exalt.	Triplicities			The Bounds of the Planets According to Ptolemy					The Faces of the Planets			De.	Fa.
			D.	N.	P.						0-10	10-20	20-30		
♈	♂+	☉ 19°	☉	♃	♄	♃ 00-06°	♀ 06-14°	☿ 14-21°	♂ 21-26°	♄ 26-30°	♂	☉	♀	♀	♄
♉	♀-	☽ 03°	♀	☽	♂	♀ 00-08°	☿ 08-15°	♃ 15-22°	♄ 22-26°	♂ 26-30°	☿	☽	♄	♂	
♊	☿+	☊ 03°	♄	☿	♃	☿ 00-07°	♃ 07-14°	♀ 14-21°	♄ 21-25°	♂ 25-30°	♃	♂	☉	♃	
♋	☽-	♃ 15°	♀ ♂	♂	☽	♂ 00-06°	♃ 06-13°	☿ 13-20°	♀ 20-27°	♄ 27-30°	♀	☿	☽	♄	♂
♌	☉+		☉	♃	♄	♄ 00-06°	☿ 06-13°	♀ 13-19°	♃ 19-25°	♂ 25-30°	♄	♃	♂	♄	
♍	☿-	☿ 15°	♀	☽	♂	☿ 00-07°	♀ 07-13°	♃ 13-18°	♄ 18-24°	♂ 24-30°	☉	♀	☿	♃	♀
♎	♀+	♄ 21°	♄	☿	♃	♄ 00-06°	♀ 06-11°	♃ 11-19°	☿ 19-24°	♂ 24-30°	☽	♄	♃	♂	☉
♏	♂-		♀ ♂	♂	☽	♂ 00-06°	♃ 06-14°	♀ 14-21°	☿ 21-27°	♄ 27-30°	♂	☉	♀	♀	☽
♐	♃+	☋ 03°	☉	♃	♄	♃ 00-08°	♀ 08-14°	☿ 14-19°	♄ 19-25°	♂ 25-30°	☿	☽	♄	☿	
♑	♄-	♂ 28°	♀	☽	♂	♀ 00-06°	☿ 06-12°	♃ 12-19°	♂ 19-25°	♄ 25-30°	♃	♂	☉	☽	♃
♒	♄+		♄	☿	♃	♄ 00-06°	☿ 06-12°	♀ 12-20°	♃ 20-25°	♂ 25-30°	♀	☿	☽	☉	
♓	♃-	♀ 27°	♀ ♂	♂	☽	♀ 00-08°	♃ 08-14°	☿ 14-20°	♂ 20-26°	♄ 26-30°	♄	♃	♂	☿	☿
	+5	+4	+3			+2					+1			-5	-4

Progressed Moon

Testing will require accurate calculations for the monthly movement of the progressed Moon. The approximate motion of the progressed Moon is 1° a month.

Declinations

Students must be able to list declinations for the progressed chart for the ACD.

Progressed House Cusps

The progressed MC can be calculated by the following methods:

- Solar Arc. Find the difference between the progressed Sun and the natal Sun. Add the result to the natal MC for the position of the progressed MC on the ACD.

- Mean Sidereal. Calculate a chart for the progressed date, using the natal time of birth.

- Meridian Arc. Add 1° for each year of age to the natal MC.

The progressed Ascendant and other progressed house cusps are interpolated from the progressed MC using a table of houses.

Solar Arc Directions

Planets and other points are directed according to the arc of the Sun (progressed Sun minus the natal Sun).

To calculate the Solar Arc, subtract the position of the natal Sun from the position of the progressed Sun as given in the ephemeris for the ACD. This will give you the Solar Arc for the ACD.

To calculate the Solar Arc for a particular age, count forward in the ephemeris one day for each year of age, starting with the birthday. From the Sun position of the resulting day, subtract the position of the Sun that is given on the birthday. The result is the Solar Arc for the age in question, on the birthday.

Antiscia (or solstice points) Singular: antiscion

Defined as the reflective position or mirror image of a given planetary position with Cancer-Capricorn as the central axis.

For example, the antiscion of 2° Cancer is 28° Gemini, and the antiscion of 3° Cancer is 27° Gemini, and so on.

The pairs of signs that reflect each other in this manner are as follows:

- Gemini-Cancer
- Taurus-Leo
- Aries-Virgo
- Pisces-Libra
- Aquarius-Scorpio
- Capricorn-Sagittarius

Earliest Predictive Techniques

The ancients used a version of directions, called primary directions, moving planets and other points a very small amount per year based on the diurnal cycle of the day of one's birth.

Planetary period or chronocrator (time-lord) systems were mostly used, whereby a planet is in charge for a long period in a person's life, within which shorter terms are co-ruled by other planets. An example is profections, which advances one sign per year for a yearly ruler, one sign per month for a monthly ruler, and even daily planetary rulers.

Other techniques include firdaria and decennials. Transits were of some small importance. Interestingly, solar returns (called "revolutions" by Lilly) have been used continuously from the beginning up to the present day.

The Asteroids and Chiron

Asteroids in common usage are Ceres, Pallas Athene, Vesta, Juno, and Chiron.

Ceres (mother—Physical nurturing, food, grain, cooking, productivity, fertility, gardening, rural life

Pallas Athene (father's daughter)—Warrior maiden, wisdom, justice, patterns, weaving, crafts, resourcefulness, urban life, cultural institutions

Vesta (sister)—Hearth and home, clannishness, safety and security, chastity, maiden aunt, vows, ritual duties

Juno (married woman)—Wife, charm, adornment, cosmetics, fashion, jealousy, victim/victimizer, relating

Chiron (centaur)—Wounded healer, mentor, primordial wisdom, high culture, ecology, traditional and alternative medicine, rape or violation, outcast, music, alternative education, stringed instruments (Chiron could not heal himself)

Fixed Stars

Fixed stars precess in the heavens and the positions given are for the year 2000.

Algol, 26° Taurus 10'—Violence, misfortune, losing one's head, suffocation, fires, artistry, music, crisis, throat ailments, neck injuries

Alcyone, 00° Gemini 00'—Largest of the Pleiades, ambitious, prominence, optimistic, eye problems, star of sorrow, exile, banishment, weeping, eye diseases

Aldebaran, 09° Gemini 47'—Royal star, courage, power, honor, popular but embattled, notoriety, intelligence, heavy losses

Sirius, 14° Cancer 05'—Brightest star, fame, riches, domestic problems, occult interests, inner vision, intense imagery, calendar star, dog bites, custodial duties, guardianship

Castor, 20° Can 14'—Keen intellect, sudden rise and honors followed by fall, distinction, hypersensitive, fondness for horses, mischievousness, intemperance, aggressiveness

South Asellus, 08° Leo 44'—Sudden downfalls, loss of reputation, seeks applause, domestic problems, hearing, speech, and mental problems, disappointments, fires, fevers, ghosts, UFOs

Regulus, 29° Leo 50'—Royal Star, honors, power, success, strong character, well-connected, ability to command, scandal, accidents

Vindemiatrix, 09° Libra 56'—Star of widowhood, cautious, inner drive for recognition, fear of poverty or failure, worry, depression, materialistic, hypocritical

Spica, 23° Libra 09'—good fortune, potential for brilliance, extraordinary talent, gifted, insight, honor, fame

Arcturus, 24° Libra 14'—Renown, self-determination, prosperity, success through slow and patient work, belligerent, quarrelsome

South Scale, 15° Scorpio 05'—Karmic debt, betrayals, loss of relatives, unforgiving, untruthful, ability to overcome hardships, clever, hidden streak of cruelty

North Scale, 19° Scorpio 22'—Star of fortune, high ambition, riches, enthusiastic, legal problems, organizational ability, highs and lows

Antares, 09° Sagittarius 46'—Royal star, great power, authority, headstrong, obstinate, gain through hard work, issues of racial and religious tolerance and human rights, suspicious, pugnacious, fires, nuclear events, exactly opposite Aldebaran

Formalhaut, 03° Pisces 09—Royal star, rise to fame or fall from grace, idealistic, mystical, visionary, lofty ideals kept pure succeed, but if corrupted for material ends, fail. Philosophical, attracted to occult.

Scheat, 29° Pisces 22'—Misfortune, suffering, love of language, erratic, grief, drowning, jealous, isolation, foot ailments, neuroses, creates own problems, artistic, floods

The Royal Stars, also called the Watchers, the Guardians, or the Four Comers of the Universe, were so called because they were used in ancient times to reckon the locations of other objects in the heavens. Each one was found at the approximate midpoint of each of the fixed constellations (Taurus, Leo, Scorpio, and Aquarius). The Royal Stars are Aldebaran (Taurus), Regulus (Leo), Antares (Scorpio), and Fomalhaut (Aquarius).

Study Guide for Level III

Review: student is responsible for all material presented in the Level I and II Guides.

Other Astrological Disciplines (See bibliography for study references)

- Uranian(Hamburg School)
- Cosmobiology
- Vedic Astrology
- Chinese Astrology
- Mesoamerican
- Classical/Ancient Astrology

THE 360° AND 90° DIALS

The 360° and 90° dials are tools for additional information and greater precision.

The 360° Dial

A metal or plastic dial, on which all 360 degrees of the zodiac are marked or numbered, is centered and secured on a blank sheet of paper.

- 0° of all four of the cardinal signs are marked as reference points with long lines and labeled.

- The positions of all points in the horoscope are marked on the paper with small lines and appropriately labeled. House cusps, as well as signs, degrees, and minutes of planets may be added.

- Once the chart is drawn, the dial is no longer held secure. It can be rotated to a wide variety of points of interest for precise measurement.

The advantages of the 360° dial over the conventional chart are:

- Both major and minor aspects in the natal chart can more easily be seen because some are indicated on the dial; and/or degrees between planets can be easily counted.

- Planetary pictures are simple to see. A planetary picture is a group of three or more planets in a symmetrical arrangement. It may consist of a pair of planets with a third planet in their midpoint or of two or more pairs of planets having a common midpoint that may or may not be occupied by a planet or point in the horoscope. Every planetary picture actually contains two midpoints forming an axis across the dial. Such an axis of a planetary picture may also be called an axis of symmetry.

Planetary Pictures

A planetary picture is found by placing the pointer on a planet and looking for equidistant planets on either side of the pointer. As stated above, it is also possible to have the midpoint unoccupied. To determine the midpoint between two planets, place the pointer between the two planets in question so that there are the same number of degrees between each planet and the pointer. If the midpoint is occupied by a planet or point or is also the midpoint of two other planets, a planetary picture is formed.

Antiscia

Antiscia (solstice points) can be easily found. Place the pointer on 0° Cancer or Capricorn (whichever is closer to the planet in question). Note the number of degrees separating the planet from 0° Cancer or Capricorn. The point at the same number of degrees on the other side of 0° Cancer or Capricorn is the antiscion of that planet.

Arabic Parts

Arabic Parts, or the sensitive points of other three-part formulas are quickly determined. The formula for all such con-

figurations is A + B - C. The pointer is placed at the midpoint of A and B and the Arabic Part or sensitive point is read from the reflective point of C.

For example, the formula for the diurnal Part of Fortune is Ascendant + Moon - Sun. Place the pointer at the midpoint of the Ascendant and the Moon (so that they are the same number of degrees on either side of the pointer). Note where the Sun is. The same number of degrees on the opposite side of the pointer is where the diurnal Part of Fortune falls. (For nocturnal births, the formula for the Part of Fortune is Ascendant + Sun - Moon).

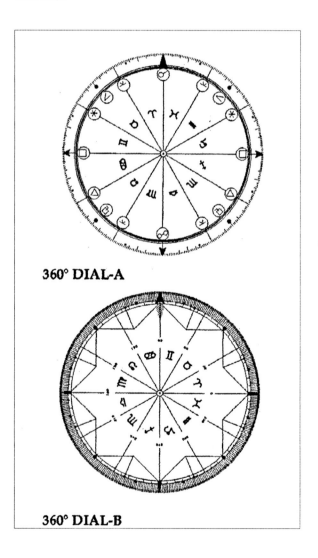

360° DIAL-A

360° DIAL-B

Transits, progressions and solar arc directions can be easily followed.

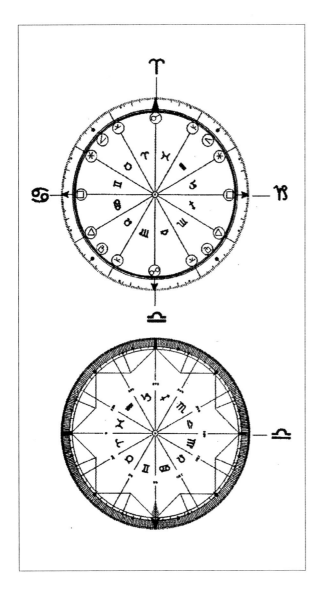

Transits

In order to find the aspects that a transiting planet is making to various points in a horoscope, the pointer of the dial is placed at the degree of the transiting planet. The chart around the dial is then scanned to determine whether the points in the horoscope are configured by any aspects that may be of interest. On some 360° dials, aspects of the twelfth harmonic (conjunction, semisextile, sextile, square, trine, quincunx, opposition) as well as the semisquare and sesquiquadrate are marked.

In addition, less easily found aspects can be quickly and accurately seen. These include the quintile (72°), the biquintile (144°), the septile (51°25.7'), biseptile (102°51.4'), triseptile (154°17.1'), and possibly others.

It is advisable at an early stage to form the habit of marking the dial itself in pencil or erasable pen at special points of interest (such as the above aspects) if they are not already marked on the dial.

Instead of examining a transit for a specific point in time, the dial can also be slowly rotated with the motion of a given

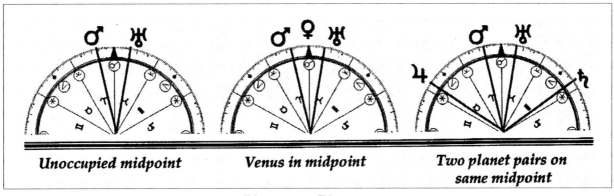

Unoccupied midpoint   Venus in midpoint   Two planet pairs on same midpoint

Planetary Pictures

planet for a particular period, noting aspects around the dial as they occur.

Progressions

Progressions can be tracked in the same manner as above for transits.

Solar Arc Directions

The solar arc of the age of interest is determined (see Level II of this study guide). Directions to and from a given planet for that age can be read by placing the pointer on the planet, noting whether any planet or point is at the number of degrees of the solar arc of interest to either side of the pointer. It is suggested that these points be marked on the dial with a pencil or erasable pen.

As described thus far, only directions by conjunction are shown. To read other aspects, place one of the two marks for the solar arc on the planet of interest, then read off aspects around the dial as described above in transits. Then repeat the procedure with the other mark.

The 90° Dial

To set up the dial, secure the dial over a blank piece of paper with 0° at the top.

Using a 90° Dial

On the paper, mark a relatively long line above the 0° point and write Aries. This represents 0° of all the cardinal signs. Place the second line at the first 30° point in a counterclockwise direction and write Taurus. This represents 0° of all the fixed signs. Place the third line on the second 30° point in a counterclock-

wise direction and write Gemini. This represents 0° of all the mutable signs.

This circle consists of 90° instead of 360°. On it the points of the conventional 360° chart are reorganized in the following manner: Points in all four cardinal signs are placed in the 0°-30° sector in the counterclockwise direction in numerical order. Continuing in a counterclockwise direction, the next 30° segment at the bottom of the chart is marked with all positions in numerical order in the fixed signs. In the final 30° segment (the upper right-hand portion of the dial) continuing in a counterclockwise direction, place all the mutable positions in numerical order.

The result is a new kind of chart on which conjunctions may represent the conjunctions found in the conventional chart but they may also represent squares and oppositions. Oppositional points on the 90° dial show both the semisquare and the sesquiquadrate.

As with the 360° dial, once the chart is drawn on the 90° dial the pointer may be rotated to any point of interest for various purposes.

The advantages of the 90° dial over the conventional chart are:

- The 90° dial focuses on the hard aspects (conjunctions, semisquares, squares, sesquiquadrates, oppositions, and also 11°15' and 22°30' aspects).

- Symmetry can be read as with the 360° dial, but with much more accuracy. In addition to the direct midpoints (conjunction and opposition point), indirect midpoints (semisquare, square, and sesquiquadrate to the conjunction and opposition point) can also be immediately seen.

- Antiscia, planetary pictures and Arabic Parts are read in exactly the same manner as with the 360° dial, but indirect as well as direct configurations of symmetry are shown.

- Transits, progressions and directions of hard aspects are read in the same manner as with the 360° dial. Other aspects may be read with the 90° dial, but less easily than with the 360° dial. With all aspects, however, the 90° dial is more precise.

There is one major difference in using the 90° dial for reading directions. When marking the dial for a given solar arc of interest, four points should be marked:

- 1. the solar arc added to the right of the 0° point on the dial;

- 2. the solar arc added to the left of the 0° point on the dial;

- 3. the solar arc added to the right of the 45° point on the dial;

- 4. the solar arc added to the left of the 45° point on the dial.

Advantages of the 360° dial over the 90° dial:

- The 360° dial can be read as a conventional chart, with intermediate house cusps indicated if desired, thus showing the house positions of the planets.

- Experiments with different house cusp positions and different house systems can easily be undertaken.

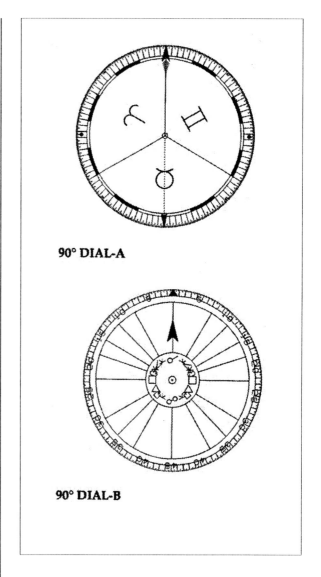

90° DIAL-A

90° DIAL-B

- The direct midpoint configurations (which are the most powerful ones) are clearly shown.

- Aspects of all harmonics can be read directly.

Advantages of the 90° dial over the 360° dial:

- The 90° dial shows primarily aspects and configurations of the 4th and 8th harmonics (hard aspects), indicating the most overt and obvious events, developments, and potentials.

- Far more precise timing and other kinds of exactness are possible with the 90° dial.

- In following solar arc directions all the major hard aspects can be read directly without having to scan the whole wheel.

- Indirect as well as direct midpoint configurations (including both midpoints and planetary pictures) can be read, although they are indistinguishable from each other.

Mundane Astrology

Mundane astrology is the branch of astrology concerned with historical and cultural trends, the study of nations and world events, meteorological conditions, and earthquakes.

Each one of these is a separate field, as follows:

- Political astrology is concerned with politically organized groups such as nations or cities.

- Astro-geology and astro-topology are concerned with the natural affinities between specific areas of Earth's surface and astrological factors.

- Historical astrology is concerned with structuring the course of history based on the astrology of cycles and world periods.

- Astro-meteorology is concerned with climate and weather fluctuations.

- Astro-seismology is concerned with earth movements and eruptions.

Techniques employed in mundane astrology include the following:

- Natal charts of politically important persons.

- Charts cast for important moments in the history of a nation, city, or community.

- Charts cast for eclipses and lunations.

- The study of major transiting phenomena.

- Cardinal ingress charts.

Horary Astrology

Horary is the branch of astrology that answers questions and forecasts the outcome of events based on a chart cast for the moment at which a question is asked, or an event takes place. The person asking the question is called the querent.

In contrast to humanistic natal astrology (in which the point of view is subjective, person-oriented, and founded on the premise that character determines destiny), horary is objective, event-oriented and founded on the premise that events determine destiny.

A planetary ruler of a house cusp signifies the matters of that house.

In horary astrology, houses describe circumstances and things.

Aspects describe relationships among the planets which in turn signify people or things.

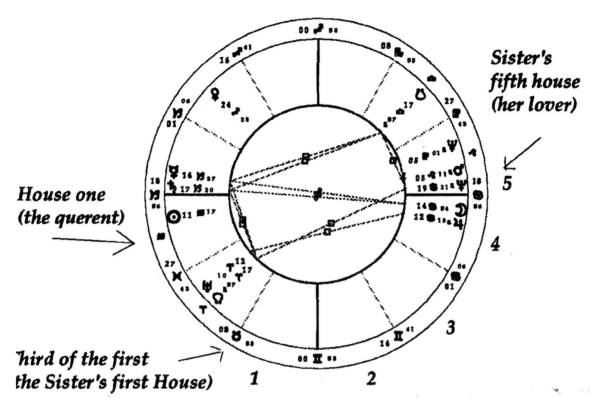

Sister's fifth house (her lover)

House one (the querent)

Third of the first (the Sister's first House)

House meanings may be described from house meanings. This is sometimes called "house of the house" or "turning the chart." For example, the client's sister's lover would be described by the seventh house—the fifth house (lovers) from the third house (brothers and sisters) of the first house (the client).

In addition to answering simple yes or no questions with horary charts, future events can be timed and the physical direction of people, places and things can be determined by the placement of significant planets in the chart.

Other terms and factors of horary astrology with which the student should become familiar are:

- Besiegement
- Impedition or Refranation
- Translation of light
- Decanates

- Peregrine planets
- Considerations against judgment
- Derived houses
- Meaning of retrograde planets.
- Use of dignities.
- Significance of fixed stars.
- Use of the Moon's Nodes, lunations, eclipses.

Inception Charts

This broadly refers to any chart that gives information based upon a given moment of time. One could say that natal astrology is also inceptional, as a person's life is read from the distinct moment of being born.

Event charts survey the exact moment of an event for a description of its meaning and outcome. They are used for large-scale occurences like earthquakes, or more personal ones like an award or a layoff notice.

A decumbiture chart is one type of event chart, the event being a person taking to his or her sick bed. It will show the timing of changes in the condition of the person and the outcome of the sickness.

Electional Astrology

Electional astrology is concerned with selecting the most favorable moment for initiating an undertaking. Electional charts can be created for such projects as the opening of a business, the timing of a wedding or partnership, and the start of a journey.

There are basically three approaches to electing a time.

- **Radical Elections**. Selecting a chart for a specific future event that is well related to the natal chart of the person (or persons) involved in the project. Natal configurations, and progressions and transits to the natal chart are used to determine a favorable time.

- **Mundane Elections**. Charts of eclipses, major conjunctions, and ingresses are used as reference points for an election. This ap-

proach is mostly considered for elections involving large groups of people.

- **Ephemeral Elections**. Only the actual transiting positions and angular relationships of the planets are considered as references.

Synastry
(Astrology of Relationships)

Interpretation of the natal charts with emphasis on relationship potential.

- Comparison—Zodiacal compatibility (signs of personal planets, elements and modes).

- Interaspects (i.e., aspects between the two charts) and important midpoints.

- Similarities and differences between the planetary dynamics of the two charts.

Composite Chart

A composite chart is a midpoint chart of two or more natal charts which describes a couple or group as a single entity.

There are two methods of erecting a composite chart:

- **Find the midpoint of the two MCs**. Look up the composite MC in a table of houses and calculate the houses for the latitude of the relationship.

- **Calculate the midpoints of all the house cusps** (the two MCs, the two 11th houses, etc.).

For either method, calculate the midpoint of each pair of planets (the two Suns, the two Moons, etc.).

Transits to planets and points in the composite chart can be used to describe developments in the relationship.

A progressed composite chart can be created by progressing each of the natal charts to a given date and calculating the midpoints of the pairs of planets and points by one of the two methods described above.

Relationship Chart

A chart calculated for the actual midpoint in time and space of two natal charts, taking into account such factors as leap years, etc. is called a relationship chart. (The new longitude and latitude may sometimes result in a highly improbable location such as the middle of the ocean).

Transits can be used to planets and points in the relationship chart.

Progressions and solar arc directions can be calculated to a particular date of interest, as with a natal chart.

The 360° and 90° Dials and Synastry

The planets and points of the two individuals involved in a relationship may be placed on a single sheet of paper using a dial, with a different color for each chart. In this way, interaspects can be easily seen.

The transits to the two charts can be tracked by placing the pointer at the po-

sition of the transiting planets and noting the aspects made to the two charts. This can be a valuable tool in timing events in the relationship.

Solar and Lunar Returns

Solar and lunar returns are transit charts calculated for the day of the return of the Sun or the Moon to its natal place. Solar returns symbolize the annual recharging and rechanneling of conscious energy. Lunar returns symbolize the monthly recharging and rechanneling of emotional energy.

The prominence of certain houses and planets in return charts indicate possible external, conscious manifestations of these energies. The natal houses so affected suggest the ultimate meaning that the experiences of the year or month will have on the life as a whole.

Solar and lunar returns are most meaningful when interpreted in light of the natal chart. Their value is extremely limited if restricted to an attempt to predict specific events. They are used most advantageously as a guide to the most productive directions the life can take within a specific time span.

A solar or lunar return may be calculated for the birthplace, the place of residence, or the place where one is on the date that the Sun returns to its natal position.

For the exam, the date and location of the return(s) to be calculated will be provided.

The History of Astrology in the West

The Ancient Middle East

Mesopotamia (today's Iraq and northeast Syria) was the birthplace of Western astrology. In this region some 4,000 years or more ago astrology evolved as a highly developed omen system utilized by a series of civilizations. It is thought that the unstable natural and political environment of the Mesopotamian region encouraged the development of a predictive system such as astrology. Mesopotamian astrology was not horoscopic; that is, it did not involve the casting of specific charts erected for a definite time, place, and date, as is done for birth charts. It was an omen-based astrology, meant for kings and princes of the region, that emphasized the conjunctions, oppositions, risings, settings and first and last visibilities of the planets and their correlations with natural phenomena and political events.

Records of astrological interpretations are found on thousands of cuneiform tablets. The earliest currently known astrological records are the Ammizaduga tablets (first Babylonian dynasty, 1645-1625 BC) which contain information on the phases of the planet Venus. The earliest known horoscope dates to 410 BC.

The stable and continuous Egyptian civilization, centered along the Nile River, was less pessimistic and fearful in outlook. The Egyptian relationship to the stars took the forms of astral-religion and sophistication in time-keeping, rather than prognostication. The tem-ples in Egypt show precise astronomical alignments. Calendar science was highly developed and eventually influenced the rest of the world. The most important astronomical event in ancient Egypt was the heliacal rising of Sirius which coincided with the flooding of the Nile, a regular and completely predictable occurrence.

(See also the section on Mesopotamian astrology in the non-Western astrology section of this Study Guide.)

Greece and Rome

Following the conquests of Alexander the Great, Middle Eastern ideas on astrology spread to Greece. The mixing of Greek geometry with Mesopotamian astrology, during what is called the Hellenistic Period, produced an elaborate body of information on horoscope reading. A significant contributor to this synthesis was Berossus, a Chaldean, who taught the Greeks astrology at his school in Cos around 280 BC. Later, Egypt emerged as the great center of astrological studies, a factor which tended to obscure astrology's earlier Mesopotamian origins. One of the earliest, and certainly the best known, astrological manual of this period was attributed to Nechepso-Petosiris, a king and his priest, in the 2nd century B.C. The oldest known work on horary and electional astrology (circa 75 AD) was written by Dorotheus of Sidon.

The Greeks also furthered the development of astronomy by speculating on the physical nature of the solar system. Ptolemy, a Greek living in Alexandria, Egypt (c.100-c.150 AD), has been considered the greatest scientist of the ancient world. His writings encompassed astronomy, geography, optics, and several other subjects. Ptolemy also wrote a short work on astrology, the *Tetrabiblos*, as well as the mathematically dense *Almagest*, an astronomical text that argued for a geocentric universe. Both books influenced Western thinking on astrology and astronomy for the next 1,500 years.

Contemporary with Ptolemy was Vettius Valens of Antioch (120-c.175 AD), a working astrologer who wrote a major work on astrology titled the *Anthology*. Unlike the scientific tone of Ptolemy's writings, Valens work is more of a casebook of applied astrology.

The Roman Empire was fertile ground for the spreading of astrology. By the time of Augustus, astrology had infiltrated nearly every aspect of Roman life. It was during this era that the poet Manilius wrote his epic poem on astrology, the *Astronomicon*. From time to time, however, charlatan astrologers filled the streets of Rome offering curbside readings. Other astrologers made predictions of when the emperor would die. These excesses led to the passing of laws to regulate the practice of astrology and also to mass expulsions of astrologers and other fortune tellers from Rome.

On a more serious level, the popular philosophy of Stoicism accepted and supported astrology. Stoicism was a philosophy of life which many leading Romans embraced, including Roman notables Cicero and Seneca. Stoic moral philosophy taught acceptance of one's fate and

Stoic metaphysics offered an explanation for the workings of astrology in a scientific sense. Astrology also reached to the highest social levels in Rome. At least two emperors were deeply involved in the subject: Tiberius employed it on a grand scale and Hadrian practiced it himself. Many consulting astrologers were among the most learned men of the time. Toward the later part of the Roman Empire, Firmicus Maternus (280-360 AD), a lawyer and senator, wrote the *Mathesis*, a textbook on the subject, most of which is still intact. In 378 AD, just a few years after Maternus, Paulus of Alexandria wrote the *Introduction*, another summary of the astrological knowledge of Roman times.

The Middle Ages

In general, the Arab civilization of the Middle Ages preserved Greek and Roman astrology and improved on certain aspects of it. The Islamic conquests brought a new political order to the Middle East and North Africa. Cultural centers such as Baghdad preserved and cultivated subjects, including classical astrology. Arabic astrology was eclectic, mundane (historical) and mathematical. The astrology of individuals, however, was not well represented. Electional, horary, and medical astrology were emphasized, thus avoiding conflicts with religious ideas on fatalism.

Among the many influential Arabic astrologers were Abu Mashar (c.787-886 AD), a leading court astrologer who was said to have authored fifty books. He is known for his writings on mundane astrology and on solar returns. Other leading Arab astrologers were Al-Kindi (c.

796-873 AD), a prolific philsophical writer on astrology, and Al-Biruni (c. 973-1048 AD) a universal scholar who was also an astronomer.

In Medieval Europe astrology as a discipline was barely preserved as an integrated body of knowledge. Early Christianity regarded astrology as pagan and discouraged its study and practice. The decline and loss of cultural centers also kept astrological interest at a very low level. Ultimately, Christian theology came to the position that natural astrology (astro-meteorology, plant and medical astrology, etc.) was entirely legitimate, but judicial astrology (natal, electional, and horary) posed some very serious problems in regard to free-will and a person's relationship to God. Astrology was discouraged, if not clearly outlawed.

By the 13th century the situation had changed. Most Italian courts had astrologers and the subject was actually being taught at the universities. The influx of Arab translations of Greek and Roman astrological works was an important element in this resurgence of interest. The astrologer Campanus (1233-1296), associated with a house system named for him, lived during this period and was a respected astronomer as well.

The theologian Thomas Aquinas, in his book *Summa Contra Gentiles*, addressed the free-will issue in astrology by stating that human mastery of the emotions can overcome the influence of the stars. Guido Bonatti (1194-1250) was one of the outstanding astrologers of the time. He taught at the University of Bologna, wrote a major textbook on astrology, and

as a consultant had many high-ranking clients.

The Renaissance

The revival of interest in antiquity fueled an interest in astrology. Philosophical traditions such as Hermeticism and Neoplatonism that supported astrology were revived and became influential. Marsilio Ficini was a leader in the translation of Arabic texts on astrology and related subjects and is now seen as a pioneer in astrological personality theory.

Printing was part of a process (the rise of the middle class) that enabled a much larger class of people to patronize astrologers. Printing also enabled a much wider dissemination of astrological concepts and tools, especially almanacs.

At the same time events such as Pico della Mirandola's attack on astrology in 1497 and a rash of failed predictions of a great flood in 1524 served to discredit astrology. (According to Thorndike's *History of Magic and Experimental Science*, 1524 was a very wet year, indeed, and there was much flood damage. The problem was that some astrologers had predicted a Noah-type flood—which of course did not happen. It appears that the 1524 flood prediction problem was less of a failure of astrology than a more persuasive influence by debunkers.) Further problems came from the Protestant movement which was hostile to astrology.

However, astrology still managed to play a major role in the science and politics of the period. Jerome Cardan (1501-1576) was a true Renaissance man—a famous intellectual and a successful astrologer. Valentin Naibod (1527-1593) authored a general treatise on astrology and advocated a measure of time used in forecasting that is named for him. John Dee (1527-1608), an English astrologer and scientist, served Queen Elizabeth I as an advisor.

The Scientific Revolution

During the Renaissance a powerful intellectual movement began, known at the time as experimental science. Stimulated by the rise of trade and the need to solve practical problems, it went on to become the dominant thought system of the modern world. Many of the pioneers and founders of modern science were also astrologers or were generally friendly toward astrology. Of these, the best known are Tycho Brahe (1534-1588) and Johannes Kepler (1571-1630). Galileo (1564-1642) did in fact cast some astrological charts, but he was also skeptical of astrology. However, the progressive nature of the scientific revolution initiated by these individuals and others quickly destroyed the Aristotelian and Ptolemaic systems, both of which served to rationalize and validate astrology.

The transition to modern science began in 1543 when Copernicus proposed that Earth revolves around the Sun. Later, Kepler refined Copernicus' system, Galileo showed that there were more things in space than could be seen with the naked eye, and Newton extended the application of mathematics to physical phenomena. The predictions made by these scientists, who at first limited their subject matter to astronomy, physics, ballistics, and optics, could not be argued with, unlike the predictions made by their contemporary astrologers. While new and convincing scientific explanations for natural phenomena were emerging, astrologers failed to organize or agree upon anything, thus insuring themselves of failure in the eyes of the new establishment.

The English Tradition

While astrology and astronomy were separating in the 17th and 18th centuries, individual practitioners of astrology such as William Lilly (1602-1681) and John Gadbury (1627-1704) flourished in England. Lilly was exceptionally well-known in his day.

He wrote *Christian Astrology*, the classic work on horary astrology, and was famous for predicting the Great Plague and the Fire of London. Many astrologers of this period published almanacs or practiced horary astrology extensively. Also, astrology for people other than the nobility became popular at this time. Attacks on astrologers increased, however, and came now from literary figures including Jonathan Swift. During this period astrology acquired a bad reputation, but the almanac with its star lore and astro-meteorlogical forecasts became a regular part of daily life; its usage has survived to the present day.

A small revival of astrology occurred in the 1780s followed by another in the mid-19th century. The latter revival included a full range of astrological offerings, from popular astrological writings that were little more than "gossip columns" to serious texts. Only a few dedicated individuals in England and America kept the astrological lights burning during this dark period in astrology's long history.

The Twentieth Century

The rise of Theosophy in England during the later part of the 19th century stimulated a major revival of astrology that was led by Sepharial (Walter Gorn Old, 1864-1929), Alan Leo (1860-1917) and others. Many consider this to have been a mixed blessing because Theosophy, with its religious overtones, was completely rejected in scientific circles. But the astrological revival was sustained on a popular level, and during the first part of the 20th century astrological groups were formed in England, Germany, and the United States.

Alfred Witte (1878-1941) founded the Hamburg School of astrology (known in the U.S. as Uranian Astrology) and produced his book *Rules for Planetary Pictures* in the 1920s. Reinhold Ebertin (1901-1988) later developed Cosmobiology, a psychologically-oriented type of astrology which utilized some of Witte's ideas and took several new directions of its own.

In 1930, newspaper astrology was born in the London Sunday Express. In Ireland, Cyril Fagan (1896-1970), a founder of the Siderealist movement in astrology, researched the ancient origins of astrology and promoted the idea and location of the sidereal zodiac. In the 1950s, Michel (1928-1991) and Francoise (1929-) Gauquelin launched the most sophisticated statistical study of astrology ever attempted, demonstrating a link between planetary position and human nature. Around this same time John Addey (1920-1982) pioneered and developed the harmonic theory of astrology.

The United States soon became a center for the revival of most schools of astrology. Evangeline Adams (1868-1932) was the first superstar astrologer and captivated America with her radio show. C.C. Zain (Elbert Benjamin, 1882-1951) published a series of influential books linking astrology with other occult sciences. Grant Lewi (1902-1951) popularized serious astrology by publishing periodicals and books. Strongly influenced by modern psychology, including the ideas of Carl Jung, the multi-talented astrologer Dane Rudhyar (1895-1985) developed what he called "humanistic astrology." Charles Jayne (1911-1985) brought a rigorous, analytical logic to the many technical problems of astrology. His cycle studies continue to be a major influence. The search for a physical mechanism that explains astrological influence was undertaken by John Nelson, an engineer who worked for RCA for many years. He developed a method to forecast geomagnetic storms that was based on heliocentric positions of planets.

Concurrent with the rise of contemporary feminism in the 1970s, Eleanor Bach produced the first ephemeris of four asteroids named for Greco-Roman goddesses and established their symbolism. Also at this time Lois Rodden (1928-2003) began to establish a rigorous rating system for horoscopic data that has set the standard in astrological research.

In the 1990s, Project Hindsight and

ARHAT, independent translation projects, began to translate numerous ancient astrological texts that had never before appeared in English and have consequently stimulated an interest in ancient astrology.

These are only some of the major contributors to astrology in the 20th century.

Mesopotamian and Non-Western Astrology

In the inhabited world of ancient times, four general regions saw the rise of great agricultural civilizations: Mesopotamia, India, China, and Mesoamerica. These four cultures produced great art, complex codes of conduct, religions, and philosophies to explain the meaning of life, as well as countless labor-saving devices that contributed to human progress. As would be expected, these civilizations had early on developed a sophisticated science of astrology/astronomy/calendrics. Successful agriculture, which requires the prediction of seasons, weather, and the counting of days, is made possible with this knowledge.

In Mesopotamia, history records the growth of cities and federations of cities along the Tigris/Euphrates Rivers. In the valley of the Indus River at places like Harappa and Mohenjo-daro, Indian civilization began. The valley of the Huang Ho (Yellow River) was the place where Chinese civilization took form, and along the Gulf of Mexico, near present day Veracruz, Mesoamerica produced its earliest cities and cultural centers. Each of these four regions tackled the challenge of conquering time in its own distinctive way and the astrological traditions that grew out of these earliest of scientific efforts are likewise unique.

Mesopotamia

As Westerners, we are most familiar with the astrological tradition of the West, one which is built on foundations laid in Mesopotamia thousands of years ago. In ancient times, skywatchers on ziggurats carefully observed the risings and settings of the Sun, Moon and planets and noted any phenomena occurring in human events that correlated with sky changes. They named the patterns of stars (the constellations) that the Sun, Moon and planets moved through and interpreted these constellations in terms of the cycle of life. Although there has been some considerable displacement between the seasons and the constellations over the past 4,000 or so years, the sequence of zodiac signs associated with the constellations correlates symbolically with the unfolding of the seasons of the year.

From ancient Mesopotamia comes our 7-day planetary week and the planetary hours of astrology. In their system of counting time, and through natural observation, the day logically served as a primary unit. But counting 365 days for the year is unwieldy, so smaller units were created. Seven days is 1/4 the roughly 28-day cycle of the Moon, and there were 7 visible planets in ancient times (including the Sun and Moon); each of the 7 days was named for a planet and was said to be ruled by it. These planetary names are found today in the romance languages; English uses the Nordic equivalents of the Roman gods associated with each planet. Each day was further divided into 24 hours, 12 for daylight and 12 for night. These were unequal hours; they varied according to the length of the day as it changes during the year. But the system was essentially astrological because the hours were ruled by the 7 planets in a definite order, the order of their average rate of motion against the sky. The 7 planets that rule the hours repeat their order 3 times during the entire day and after 21 hours a new cycle begins, starting with another planet in the sequence. Whichever planet rules the first hour of the day, the hour after sunrise, gave its name to that day—hence, the names of the days and the sequential order of planets for the week are set. The system of planetary hours puts forth an astrology that names, and consequently gives meaning to blocks of time. This same concept of planetary influence on time periods appeared in ancient China and Mesoamerica and formed the core of their astrological systems.

The astrology of Mesopotamia was an astrology also concerned with sky omens, especially those associated with the planets. Conjunctions and oppositions were observed in the clear, unobstructed skies of the ancient Middle East. Planets on the horizon, just rising or setting, were studied; this emphasis survives as the Ascendant and Descendant points in the modern Western astrological chart. When the Greeks rose to power in the region, they began to geometricize Mesopotamian astrology until it became almost entirely spatial. They added aspects, house divisions, and made the ecliptic-based 12-sign zodiac the showpiece of the system. Although much of what they did was built on older ideas, to them must go the credit for constructing a more rigorous system.

By Roman times, astrology was a specialized discipline with a clear-cut methodology, described in books and practiced by experts. Today, this tradition is still very much alive and constantly evolving.

India

In ancient India, skywatchers also learned to make calendars and predict where planets would be in the future. The Vedas, the sacred writings of ancient India, reveal a sky-knowledge that dates back to very early times. In 323 BC Alexander the Great extended his empire into parts of India and opened the flood gates for an exchange of cultures. Greco-Mesopotamian astrology found its way into India and influenced the form that Indian astrology eventually took. By the 5th century AD the first Indian astrological treatises appeared. Parashara authored the first major astrological text, *Hora Sastra*, which strongly influenced later Vedic astrological writings. By the time the great 6th century Indian astrologer Vaharamihira published his masterwork on astrology, the *Brihat Jataka*, the distinctive elements of Indian astrology were in place: a blend of ancient Vedic and Greco-Mesopotamian astrology.

Today, Vedic astrology seems to be the preferred term for the indigenous astrology of India, the term obviously referring to the Vedas. In the recent past it has also been known as Indian or Hindu astrology. The Indian name for the study of both astronomy and astrology is

Jyotish. In India, *Jyotish* is taught in universities and practiced by professionals.

The exchange with Western astrology brought in the 12-sign zodiac, but in India its first point became attached to the constellation Aries, not the vernal equinox as has become the tradition in the West. Indian astrologers practice a sidereal astrology, placing the planets in signs that use the same names as in Western astrology, but are displaced from that zodiac by about 24 degrees. The distance between the two is called the *Ayanamsa*, a distance that is set officially by the government astrologer in India, although there is still debate among experts who use different figures.

The signs in Vedic astrology are called *Rasis*. The horoscope used in India, called the *Rasi Chakra*, is very similar to the square charts used by astrologers in Roman and Medieval times. Like Western astrology, Indian astrology became quite spatial and aspects and house positions are fundamental to the system.

Although very wide orbs are used in Vedic astrology when interpreting aspects, other techniques are employed that reveal subtle details about the distribution of the planets in the zodiac. Each zodiac sign is divided into thirds, fifths, sixths, sevenths, eighths, ninths, etc. A chart called the *navamsa* chart, based on a division of signs into ninths, is commonly used in modern Vedic astrology to analyze marriage and relationships. It is also said to reveal one's deeper spiritual tendencies in addition to marriage

karma. Essentially, this chart is a 9th harmonic chart and it treats novile aspects (a minor aspect of 40 degrees that most Western astrologers ignore) as conjunctions.

In India, one's Ascendant, called the *Lagna*, is considered the strongest point of personal identity. The Moon's nodes also play an important role in Vedic astrology: *Rahu* is the name for the north node, *Ketu* is the name for the south node. The Sanskrit names for the planets are as follows: Sun = *Ravi*; Moon = *Chandra*; Mercury = *Budha*; Venus = *Sukra*; Mars = *Kuja*; Jupiter = *Guru*; Saturn = *Sani*.

One unique and probably indigenous element in Indian astrology is found in the *Nakshatras*, the 27 lunar mansions, or signs of the Moon. These are each $13°20'$ in length and begin at the first point of Aries. (Western, Chinese and Arabian astrological traditions contain what are often called lunar mansions or a lunar zodiac. In these systems the ecliptic is generally divided into 28 sections, each measuring $12°51'$.

Vedic astrology also has a system of 28 lunar mansions that are normally reserved for use in horary and electional astrology). The *Nakshatra* in which the Moon at birth is found is the foundation for perhaps the most interesting technique in Indian astrology, the computation of the *Dasas*. In this forecasting technique, the spatial position of the Moon determines a sequence of time periods that affect the native throughout the course of life. In other words, space is turned into time. The Dasas are time-periods, blocks of symbolic time.

China

India was certainly influenced by Greco-Mesopotamian culture, but China, far more isolated, was much less so. In China, astrology took on forms very different from those in the West. The planets plus the Sun and Moon were not measured against the ecliptic-based zodiac; they were measured against the equator. The pole star was a point of great importance to the Chinese and it is the celestial equator, not the ecliptic, that relates to this point. Twenty-eight unequal lunar mansions on the equator, called *Hsiu*, divided the sky. The position of the Moon in each of these zones acquired a meaning. But this is about as far as Chinese positional or spatial astrology went. The real core of the system lies in an interplay of time cycles that may have originally been based on a combination of numerology and astronomical motions.

In very ancient times the *Ten Celestial Stems*, a sequence of ten consecutive symbols, became established as a symbolic cycle. Its most ancient origins may lie in the counting of fingers on two hands, or it may possibly also be a surviving artifact of an ancient 10-day week. Later the *Twelve Terrestrial Branches*, another symbolic cycle of stages—perhaps influenced by both the 12-year cycle of Jupiter and the division of the solar year into 12ths—was combined with the ten Stems to create a cycle of 60 days or 60 years. In a 60-day or 60-year period there are six cycles of the Stems and five cycles of the Branches. Each day or year in the cycle would then have two names, one for the Stem, one for the Branch. This sexagenary cycle applied to years is said to have been created by the legendary emperor Huang Ti in the year 2677 BC.

This same interplay of ten and twelve, using the same names, was also applied to months and hours. In the case of months, one year will, with fancy adjustments, contain 12 months and so five years will yield 60 months. In terms of hours, five days of 12 hours each gives us the number 60 again. The year, month, day and hour of one's birth, the *Four Pillars of Destiny* as they are called, are then designated by a pair of names. Associations with the five elements of Chinese astrology (fire, earth, metal, water, and wood) and the polarities (yin and yang) further individualize the information about the birth moment. Today, Chinese astrologers still utilize this ancient system and almanacs are regularly published containing tables for determining the astrological qualities of any given day.

A full Chinese astrological reading takes into consideration more than just the Four Pillars of Destiny. The 28 lunar mansions or constellations are said to rule a day each, such that every four weeks of seven days begins the cycle anew. These constellations are said to indicate the element of chance and are used not only in interpreting a birth, but also for choosing auspicious days.

Another factor considered in a reading is the animal that rules the year of birth. This is a cycle of twelve years (not to be confused with the Twelve Terrestrial Branches), each year named for an animal and beginning with the Chinese New Year in early February. It is thought that this 12-year cycle is based on the cycle of Jupiter. The influence of the year of birth is said to denote the moral character of the person. This aspect of Chinese astrology has become quite popular in the Western world, but as we have seen, it is in reality only a small portion of a complex system.

Mesoamerica

We now come to the fourth, and least known, of the world's great astrological traditions, the time-based astrology of Mesoamerica. Around the time of the ancient Greeks (800 to 200 BC) a civilization, known today as the Olmec, was flourishing along the eastern coast of today's Mexico. Forerunners of the Maya, Toltecs, and Aztecs, the Olmecs built pyramids and ceremonial centers and also created a complex astro-calendrical system, portions of which have survived to the present day. During the Classic period of the Maya, when Europe was in its Dark Ages, this system evolved into one of the world's most sophisticated intellectual constructions. Scholars have long marveled at the precision achieved by the Maya in measuring the year and the cycles of the Moon. The purpose of all this astronomy was, however, to improve their astrology.

The Maya, Toltecs, Aztecs and other pre-Columbian cultures of Mesoamerica based their astrological analyses on the interplay of day-counts, not unlike the Chinese. They used a cycle of 13 numbers and a cycle of 20 signs which interfaced every 260 days as the core of their system. Also like the Chinese, they projected this cycle onto a larger frame of reference, dividing their creation cycle of 5,125 years (also called the Long Count)

into 260 units of 7,200 days called *katuns*. The present creation cycle is due to end on December 21, 2012. On April 6, 1993, the last, or 260th katun of the series that originated in 3114 BC began. Note that the Mayan creation cycle of 5,125 years is exactly 1/5th of the average cycle of Earth's precession, the movement that accounts for the shifting of the astrological ages described in Western astrology.

The key concept in Mesoamerican astrology is the notion of time as a sign. As we have already seen, the astrology of the West is mostly spatial. The most important yardstick in that system is determined by the signs of the zodiac, each sign measuring 30 degrees of space along the ecliptic. The astrological houses and the aspects are also spatial. A conjunction of planets or an eclipse is interpreted according to the sign in which it occurs. In ancient Mexico, however, astrologers interpreted a conjunction or an eclipse according to the 13-day sign in which it occurred, as well as other symbolic time frames.

Perhaps the most carefully watched planet in ancient Mesoamerica was Venus. Its 584-day synodic cycle was divided into four periods: inferior conjunction, morning star, superior conjunction, and evening star. The two appearance intervals of Venus—morning star and evening star—each last for 263 days on average. It has been suggested that this is one of several astronomical facts behind the selection of 260 as a master number in Mesoamerican astrology. Throughout Mesoamerica it was believed that when Venus was conjunct the Sun and moving retrograde (the inferior conjunction), leaders would be struck down and there would be trouble in the land. The motions of Venus were recorded in books in the form of complex, and very accurate tables. The Maya were well aware that five synodic cycles of Venus are equal to eight solar years and this knowledge formed an important part of their astrological-cosmological symbolism.

In terms of a horoscope for a birth, Mesoamerican astrology was similar to Chinese astrology. There was no circular chart as such, just a list of factors that needed to be considered in the analysis of character and destiny. First came the year of birth, one of four signs that were part of a 52-year cycle. Next were the 20 day-signs and the 13-day periods into which the birth fell. The Day-Sign, perhaps the most important and personal of the significators, was studied closely; it was often used as a part of a person's name. Each of these 20 signs was linked to one of the four directions, which function in many ways like the four elements in Western astrology. The ruler of the hour of birth and the phases of the Moon and Venus extended the interpretation. For mundane events, such as dedications and coronations, the stations of Mars, Jupiter, and Saturn were considered important factors in the quality of any given day.

Because the Spanish friars did a thorough job of eliminating anything they saw as pagan, we are not completely sure about the factors included in a traditional Mesoamerican astrological reading. What we do know of this great tradition is based mostly on the works of archaeoastronomers and anthropologists. However, in remote parts of Mexico and Guatamala, an oral tradition that retains some of the ancient astrological knowledge has survived and is becoming better organized and more resistant to the constant pressures from Christianity. Academic researchers, practicing what they call ethnoastronomy, are also recording and documenting pieces of this lost knowledge.

Study Guide for Level IV

Rectification

All candidates for Level IV certification must rectify a chart before starting their chosen track (consulting, general research or statistical research). Candidates may either select a chart of their choice, or request that one be assigned and sent to them.

If the choice is to have a chart assigned, the candidate should send the request and a $90 check (made payable to NCGR) to the National Education Director. Birth data (date and place of birth) will be sent along with a biography and at least 6 major events in the life. The candidate's name should not appear on any papers submitted. The National Education Director will assign a code number.

IF THE CANDIDATE CHOOSES AN ASSIGNED RECTIFICATION, IT SHOULD BE RETURNED TO THE NATIONAL EDUCATION DIRECTOR WITHIN 60 DAYS.

If the candidate chooses to select the chart to be rectified, upon completion of the rectification all the materials pertaining to it should be sent with a self-assigned code number, along with the fee to the National Education director.

In either case the defense will consist of the following, the written parts of which are to be typed and double-spaced:

1. a one-page copy of the biography, including six to ten events with dates.

2. a two-page explanation of your rectification procedure, listing the techniques that you used. This must include at least three different timing techniques such as transits, secondary progressions, solar arc directions, eclipses, etc. Be sure to indicate all the main steps in the process from beginning to end.

3. a three to fifteen page defense of how you arrived at your result. At least two of the techniques chosen should be applied to each of the six events. They need not be the same ones for all events.

4. a one to three page description of how your chart fits the biographical sketch.

5. a rectified chart with date, time and place of birth.

Each statement of evidence for the accuracy of the rectified chart must include the following information: AspectING body/point, zodiacal position; aspectED (natal, progressed, relocated, etc.) body/point, zodiacal position; orb; declination.

For example: Divorce, September 19, 1965

Transiting Uranus (15° Virgo 22') square natal Ascendant (15° Gemini 28'), orb of 6 minutes

Uranus (often referred to as "the planet of divorce") symbolizes radical or drastic change often in the form of a reversal aspecting the Ascendant (which is the partnership axis).

Copies of all charts (or listings) necessary to accomplish and judge the rectification must be included. For example, progressed charts (or listings) in support of progressed positions cited, listing of all solar arcs when applicable, relocation charts, charts of significant other persons where synastry is used.

Once the rectification is passed the candidate has the option of taking any (or all) certifications. One is for consulting, another for technical research and the third for general research. Upon passing all requirements the candidate will receive a document suitable for framing which will appropriately recognize and certify the candidate's achievement.

Examination for Professional Research Astrologer: Scientific, Technical, Statistical Option

General description: exploration of areas of astrology utilizing generally accepted scientific (physical or social) and/or statistical methods.

First, a proposal must be submitted to the National Education Director along with a check for $50 made payable to NCGR Education. Also include verification that you have passed the rectification requirement for Level IV and that you would like to take the Resarch Track, Scientific, Technical, Statistical Option. The proposal should include:

- Proposed topic (50 to 100 words)
- Proposed hypotheses (50 to 100 words)
- Proposed methodology (50 to 100 words)

You will be notified of acceptance, conditional acceptance or rejection. You can proceed to research the topic as agreed upon.

The final result should be a research paper of no less than 15 pages, nor more than 40 pages (typewritten and double-spaced) in length (exceptions for special reasons may be granted). In this paper you are expected to state hypotheses and methodology clearly, as well as meaningful results, be they negative or positive.

For the conventions of manuscript preparation, footnotes, bibliography, etc., it may be helpful to refer to the *MLA Style*

Manual (Joseph Gibaldi, 1998, Modern Language Association, www.mla.org.).

Two copies of the paper must be submitted to the National Education Director. The National Education Director will inform you of acceptance, conditional acceptance or rejection. The local Education Chairperson (where applicable) will also be notified.

Examination for Professional Research Astrology: General Studies Option

General description: exploration of less rigorously defined areas of astrology such as case studies or interpretive approaches and symbolism. In many cases methods and materials may be drawn from those academic disciplines known as the humanities—such as psychology, history, philosophy, literature, the arts, philology, mythology.

First, a proposal must be submitted to the National Education Director along with a check for $50 made payable to NCGR Education. Also include verification that you have passed the rectification requirement for Level IV and that you would like to take the Research Track, General Studies Option. The proposal should include:

Proposed topic and reasons for choice (50 to 100 words)

Proposed line of investigation (50 to 100 words)

List 5-15 most essential texts and references for your topic, if applicable

You will be notified of acceptance, conditional acceptance or rejection. You can proceed to research the topic as agreed upon.

Guidelines for the General Research Track

1. Hypotheses

What are the questions being asked in the project?

What is already known about the topic? (Review of principle literature on the subject.)

State the practical or philosophical value of the study.

2. Project design

State the sources of information that will be consulted to support this study.

Describe guidelines and procedure you plan to follow.

3. Results

Conclusions should be relevant to the original objective of the study.

Describe the contribution this study makes to the knowledge of the field.

If your conclusions contradict generally accepted assumptions, defend your position.

The final result should be a research paper of no less than 15 pages, nor more than 35 pages (typewritten and double-spaced) in length (exceptions for special reasons may be granted). In this paper you are expected to state hypotheses and methodology clearly, as well as meaningful results, be they negative or positive.

For the conventions of manuscript preparation, footnotes, bibliography, etc., it may be helpful to refer to the *MLA Style Manual* (Joseph Gibaldi, 1998, Modern Language Association, www.mla.org.).

Two copies of the paper must be submitted to the National Education Director. The National Education Director will inform you of acceptance, conditional acceptance or rejection. The local Education Chairperson (where applicable) will also be notified.

Examination for the Professional Consulting Astrologer

Application and Procedure

To apply for this examination, send a resume to the Education Director, stating what counseling knowledge/experience you may have. Along with your letter enclose a check for $75 made payable to NCGR Education. Your out-of-pocket cost will be $50 after the client pays you $25. Also include verification that you have passed the rectification requirement for Level IV and that you would like to take the Consulting Track.

As you apply, please have two written character references sent to the National Education Director. Both letters should be from individuals who know you in an area of life unrelated to astrology. References from relatives cannot be accepted.

After receipt of your application and examination fee you will be notified that the client has agreed to contact you directly and pay you a fee of $25. You also have the option of selection of your own client. You will then proceed as you would with any professional relationship.

As part of the examination, you are required to record and submit two 90-minute cassettes of the session. The client will also be informed of this procedure and its purpose as an evaluation tool for your candidacy as a professional consulting astrologer. You may wish to suggest to the client that he or she has the option of taping the session as well; the client should then bring along a separate recorder and cassette for this purpose.

In certain special cases, such as an applicant who lives in a remote area where it would be difficult for the Education Director to find a client living near you, you may either conduct this test with a phone consultation for which an Education Director will supply the client, or you may submit the names and phone numbers of three individuals known to you (not relatives or close friends) whom you have queried as to their willingness to possibly participate. The Education Director will then contact and arrange for one of them to be your client. You will then proceed as you would with any professional relationship.

The Examination

There are three sections to the examination:

1. Preparation for the consulting session.

2. The consulting session. (Natal plus projection for at least 6 months.)

3. Your critique of the session.

Sections 1 and 3 are to be presented as written commentaries; Section 2 is to be presented as one 90-minute cassette.

DO NOT IDENTIFY YOURSELF on any materials except by the code number assigned to you by the National Education Director.

Furthermore, every effort will be made to protect the client's identity. Therefore, on the materials you submit, the client's name should not be revealed. Only you, the client, your local Education Chairperson, and the National Education Director are to know the client's identity. (A first name alone is unlikely to reveal the client's identity on the cassette.)

Preparation for the Consulting Session

After you have studied the chart but before you see the client, please prepare:

1. Copies of the charts and any other technical materials you normally use.

2. A written analysis of your understanding and expectations of the client; and how you would handle any sensitive is-

sues that could arise based on these expectations. Be sure to justify your remarks with the astrological indications which lead to your judgments. (Maximum of 10 pages, no less than 5 pages, typed and double-spaced.)

3. A written essay as follows:

Relying on your own personal value system, describe what you consider to be your professional and ethical standards as a consulting astrologer, addressing the topics listed below. Please respond to each topic with a paragraph or two. The purpose of this essay is to help you define and clarify your thinking about professional and ethical issues. There are not necessarily any right or wrong answers. You will be evaluated only on how well you defend your positions.

1. Client confidentiality

2. Privacy and appropriateness of session location and setting

3. Maintaining time structure of session

4. Establishing fees

5. Setting a cancellation/lateness policy

6. Allowing another person (or persons) to be present at the session.

7. Predicting death or serious illness of client/or a client's loved one

8. The suitability and use of astrological jargon

9. Friendships with clients outside the session

10. Emotional involvement with client within the session

Two typed copies of both the written analysis and the written essay must be mailed to the National Education Director and postmarked before you meet the client.

Consulting Session

Record the consulting session on cassette. (Please use one 90-minute cassette even though the session may run shorter.)

Post-Consultation Critique

Following the session, please prepare a written evaluation of the client, the events of the session and your own performance. This should be based both on the chart and your experience of the session. This is also an opportunity to comment on matters you chose not to cover during the recording of the session.

The critique should be no less than 5 and no longer than 10 typed, double-spaced pages.

Two copies of the cassette and two copies of the post-consultation critique and all other paperwork must be mailed to the National Education Director and postmarked within a week after the consultation.

Examiners and Criteria for Judgment

The National Education Director will submit your written materials and cassette to two examiners who do not live in your geographical location.

Two examiners receive candidates materials simultaneously. If they both agree, their decision stands. However, if one passes the candidate and one fails, the tape and papers go to a third examiner, whose judgment will be the tie-breaker.

Your identity will not be revealed to the examiners. Their identities will not be revealed to you.

Your skill and wisdom in consulting, your ability to synthesize, your flexibility in meeting the reality of the client, and your technical expertise will be the examiners' criteria for judgment.

Consultations are not to be a mere recitation of educational information about everything in the client's chart. You are not teaching a class; you are conducting a consultation in which the client's needs are paramount. Wisdom in consulting requires skill beyond knowledge of astrological technique. The criteria of judgment for the examiners evaluating your tape will include your ability to listen effectively as well as speak, to synthesize information and to be flexible in meeting the reality of your client in an ethical and responsible manner.

The National Education Director will inform you and your local Education Chairperson of the examiners' decision.

Examination for Professional Instructor in Astrology

The candidate is to provide:

1. A curriculum for one course in astrol-

ogy, including:

A. Scope (what will be covered in the course) and sequence (how it fits in with the broader educational programs of learning astrology).

b. Syllabus

c. Booklist

d. Reading, homework assignments and lesson plans for each lesson in the course.

e. List what materials will be used in class (handouts, etc..)

f. How students will be evaluated.

g. The business side—how the instructor will cultivate students, what pricing will be used and how the instructor will be compensated, where classes will be held and what kind of structure will be established for students (contracts, appication forms, etc.)?

2. In-depth materials for one class, including:

a. A tape of one's verbal presentation, 90-120 minutes in length. (Another form of proof of one's efficacy in presenting may be possible, but a proposal for such must be submitted to the Board of Examiners for approval).

b. A detailed outline/plan for the class

c. Copies of handouts or overhead transparencies to be used in class.

(Masters for transparencies, rather than actual transparencies are acceptable.)

d. Homework and reading assignments, if any.

e. A brief explanation of how everything associated with the class relates to:

i. Its plan and purpose

ii. Its role in the scope and sequence of the course of which it is a part

iii. If it is a separate unit itself (such as a stand-alone workshop), what benefit it provides the student.

f. A critique of the presentation after the class is taught. (3-5 pages typewritten) in terms of its:

i. Organization

ii. Effectiveness in teaching the student

iii. How well the ancillary materials worked to support the intended purpose of the class

iv. How the class might be improved.

Examiners and Criteria for Judgment

The National Education Director will submit your written materials and cassette to two examiners who do not live in your geographical location. Your identity will not be revealed to them. Their identities will not be revealed to you.

In the event of conflicting judgments, your examination will be submitted to a third examiner.

Your skill and wisdom in preparation, your ability to present the material to the class, your flexibility in meeting the reality of the classroom environment and feedback from students, and your technical expertise will be the examiners' criteria for judgment.

A National Education Director will inform you of the examiners' decision.

Bibliography

Books introduced under the heading of one level are not repeated on successive levels. It should be assumed that the book recommendations are cumulative. Preparation for each level assumes familiarity with material from prior levels.

All books on this list were verified as available as of September 2003 through Internet searches of one or more the following sites:

- www.allbookstores.com
- www.astrologyetal.com

- www.astroamerica.com
- www.amazon.com

In the case of a few self-published titles, information source is as specified with the entry.

The subject of **Ethics** for astrologers is introduced at Level I and incorporated into testing for all levels. At the end of this bibliography, following the book recommendations for Consulting Track, is a list of recommended articles on ethics. Following that, the entire **NCGR Code of Ethics** is printed.

Bibliography, Level I

Ephemerides

The American Ephemeris series, ACS Publications. Compiled and programmed by Neil F. Michelsen, with updates on newer editions by Rique Pottenger.

The American Ephemeris for the 20th Century, midnight or noon versions.

The American Ephemeris for the 21st Century, midnight or noon versions.

The American Ephemeris, 2000-2010. Earlier decades also available.

All decade ephemerides include declinations and aspectarians.

The American Heliocentric Ephemeris, 2001-2050.

The American Sidereal Ephemeris, 2001-2025.

The Astrolabe World Ephemeris, 2001-2050, Midnight. Whitford Press.

The Rosicrucian Ephemeris, 1900-2000, Midnight. Rosicrucian Fellowship.

Michelsen, Neil F., with revisions by Rique Pottenger, *Tables of Planetary Phenomena, Second Edition.* ACS Publications. Ephemerides of numerous phenomena, such as eclipses, ingresses, planetary distances, stations, clusters, lunar phases, etc.

Tables of Houses

The Michelsen Book of Tables, compiled by Neil F. Michelsen. Tables for both Placidus and Koch houses, plus diurnal motion, logarithm tables, timetables, and step-by-step instructions on erecting a horoscope. ACS Publications.

Placidus Table of Houses. Rosicrucian Fellowship.

Table of Houses, Koch System. AstroNumeric/AFA.

Table of Houses, Placidus System. AstroNumeric/AFA.

Longitudes, Latitudes, and Time Changes

The American Atlas, Expanded Fifth Edition. Compiled and programmed by Thomas Shanks. ACS Publications.

The International Atlas, Revised Fifth Edition. Compiled and programmed by Thomas Shanks. ACS Publications.

Reference: Dictionaries, Rulerships, Encyclopedias

Bills, Rex. *The Rulership Book.* AFA.

Brau, Jean-Louis, Helen Weaver, and Allan Edmands, eds. *Larousse Encyclopedia of Astrology.* McGraw-Hill Book Company.

Carter, C.E.O. *An Encyclopedia of Psychological Astrology.* Astrology Classics.

DeVore, Nicholas. *Encyclopedia of Astrology.* Astrology Classics.

Gettings, Fred. *The Arkana Dictionary of Astrology, revised edition.* Penguin Arkana.

Lehman, J. Lee, Ph.D. *The Book of Rulerships: Keywords from Classical Astrology.* Whitford Press.

Lehman, J. Lee, Ph.D. *Essential Dignities.* Whitford Press.

Lewis, James R. *The Astrology Encyclopedia.* Visible Ink.

Munkasey, Michael. *Astrological Thesaurus,* available as a CD from www.astrocollege.com.

Munkasey, Michael. *The Concept Dictionary.* Arcturus, (limited availability, listed with www.astroamerica.com.)

Chart Collections

Dodson, Carolyn. *Horoscopes of the US: States and Cities.* AFA.

Penfield, Marc. *Horoscopes of the USA & Canada.* AFA.

Rodden, Lois M. *Astro-Data I: Profiles of Women.* Data News.

Rodden, Lois M. *Astro-Data II* (formerly *American Book of Charts*). AFA.

Rodden, Lois M. *Astro-Data III* (may be out-of-print). AFA.

Rodden, Lois M. *Astro-Data IV.* (musicians, designers, architects, authors, poets, dancers, and singers). AFA.

Rodden, Lois M. *Astro-Data V: Profiles in Crime.* Data News.

Where to Write for Vital Records, 2nd Edition. Consumer Education Research Center.

Where to Write for Vital Records. Berman Associates.

Online source for data and charts: www.astrodatabank.com

Online source for vital records: www.vitalchek.com

Astronomy

Filbey, John and Peter Filbey. *Astronomy for Astrologers.* (out-of-print, limited availability).

Heath, Robin. *Sun, Moon, Earth.* Walker & Co.

Mayo, Jeff. *The Astrologer's Astronomical Handbook.* (out-of-print, limited availability).

Introductory Texts

Arroyo, Stephen. *Astrology, Psychology, and the Four Elements.* CRCS Publications.

Banzhaf, Hajo and Anna Haebler. *Key Words for Astrology.* Samuel Weiser.

Burk, Kevin. *Understanding the Birth Chart.* Llewellyn.

Burt, Kathleen. *Archetypes of the Zodiac.* Llewellyn

Davison, Ronald C. *Astrology: The Classic Guide to Understanding Your Horoscope.* CRCS Publications.

Forrest, Steven. *The Inner Sky.* ACS Publications.

Kempton-Smith, Debbi, *Secrets from a*

Stargazer's Notebook, Topquark.

Lamb, Terry. *Beginning Astrology Math Workbook*. NCGR.

March, Marion D. and Joan McEvers. *The Only Way to Learn Astrology, Vol. I: Basic Principles*. ACS Publications.

March, Marion D. and Joan McEvers. *The Only Way to Learn Astrology, Vol. II: Math & Interpretation Techniques*. ACS Publications.

Maynard, Jim. *The Pocket Astrologer*. Quicksilver Productions.

Negus, Joan, *Basic Astrology: A Guide for Teachers and Students*. ACS Publications (out-of-print, limited availability).

Negus, Joan. *Cosmic Combinations*. ACS Publications (out-of-print, limited availability)

Oken, Alan. *Complete Astrology*. Bantam

Parker, Julia and Derek Parker. *Parker's Astrology*. Dorling Kindersley.

Pottenger, Maritha. *Easy Astrology Guide*. ACS Publications.

Rogers-Gallagher, Kim. *Astrology for the Light Side of the Brain*. ACS Publications.

Sasportas, Howard. *The Twelve Houses*. Aquarian Press (out of print, limited availability).

Soffer, Shirley. *The Astrology Sourcebook: A Guide to the Symbolic Language of the Stars*. McGraw-Hill Book Company

Books Helpful for Interpretation

Barz, Ellynor. *Gods and Planets: The Archetypes of Astrology*. Chiron Publications.

Burk, Kevin. *Astrology: A Comprehensive Guide to Classical Interpretation*. Llewellyn Publications.

Carter, C.E.O. *The Astrological Aspects*. AFA.

Dobyns, Zipporah. *Finding the Person in the Horoscope*. TIA Publications.

Greene, Liz. *Saturn*. Red Wheel/Samuel Weiser.

Guttman, Ariel and Kenneth Johnson. *Mythic Astrology: Archetypal Powers in the Horoscope*. Llewellyn.

Hand, Robert. *Planets in Youth: Patterns of Early Development*. Whitford Press.

Jayne, Vivia. *Aspects to Horoscope Angles*. AFA

Jayne, Vivia. *By Your Lights*. AFA.

Jones, Marc Edmund. *The Guide to Horoscope Interpretation*. Theosophical Publishing House.

Lewi, Grant. *Astrology for the Millions*. Llewellyn Publications.

Lewi, Grant. *Heaven Knows What*. Llewellyn Publications.

Marks, Tracy. *The Art of Chart Interpretation*. CRCS Publications.

Marks, Tracy. *Planetary Aspects: Making Your Stressful Aspects Work for You*. CRCS Publications.

Rudyhar, Dane. *The Astrological Houses: The Spectrum of Individual Experience*. Random House Publishers.

Simms, Maria Kay. *Your Magical Child*. ACS Publications.

Spiller, Jan. *Astrology for the Soul*. Bantam.

Stanley, Ena. *Astrology's Basics: Examining the Chart's Structure*, available on CD from www.astrocollege.com or Amazon.com.

Stanley, Ena, *The Archetypes: Unlocking the Mysteries of the Planets, Signs and Houses*, available on CD from www.astrocollege.com or Amazon.com.

Tierney, Bil. *The Dynamics of Aspect Analysis*. CRCS Publications.

Tompkins, Sue. *Aspects in Astrology*. Inner Traditions International, Ltd.

Van Toen, Donna. *The Astrologer's Node Book*. Red Wheel/Weiser.

Bibliography, Level II

General and Miscellaneous

Arroyo, Stephen. *Astrology, Karma, and Transformation*. CRCS Publications.

Ashman, Bernie. *Roadmap to your Future*. ACS Publications.

Campion, Nicholas. *The Practical Astrologer*. Hamlin. Order from Amazon.co.uk.

Crane, Joseph. *A Practical Guide to Traditional Astrology*. A.R.H.A.T.

Dobyns, Zipporah. *The Node Book*. TIA Publications.

Ebertin, Reinhold. *Applied Cosmobiology*. Ebertin-Verlag.

Essentials of Intermediate Astrology, anthology of articles on Level II material, NCGR, www.geocosmic.org

Filbey, John and Peter Filbey. *The Astrologer's Companion*. Borgo Pr. (out of print, limited availability).

Forrest, Steven. *The Night Speaks*. ACS Publications.

Hand, Robert. *Horoscope Symbols*. Schiffer Publishing.

Hand, Robert. *Night and Day: Planetary Sect in Astrology*. A.R.H.A.T.

Henson, Donna. *The Vertex*. AFA

Jayne, Charles. *Best of Charles Jayne*. AFA.

Lamb, Terry. *Cycles of Childhood*. (Monogram). NCGR.

Lehman, J. Lee, Ph.D. *Classical Astrology for Modern Living*. Whitford Press.

Mann, A.T. *The Round Art*. Vega Books. Order from Amazon.co.uk.

March, Marion D. and Joan McEvers. *The Only Way to Learn Astrology, Vol. III: Horoscope Analysis*. ACS Publications.

Meyer, Michael R. *Humanistic Astrology Revisited: 1997 Special Edition*.

Pottinger, Maritha. *Astrology, The Next Step*. ACS Publications.

Pottinger, Maritha. *The East Point and the Antivertex*. ACS Publications.

Ruperti, Alexander. *Cycles of Becoming*. CRCS (out-of-print, limited availability)

Sakoian, Frances and Louis S. Acker. *The Astrologer's Handbook*. Harper & Row.

Tebbs, Carol, *Beyond Basics: Moving the Chart in Time*, available on CD from www.astrocollege.com or Amazon.com

Westin, Leigh. *Declinations*. Self-published. Available from www.astrocollege.com

Lunar and Planetary Phases

George, Demetra. *Finding Our Way Through the Dark*. ACS Publications.

Robertson, Marc. *Not a Sign in the Sky but a Living Person*. Astrology Center of the Northwest.

Rudhyar, Dane. *The Lunation Cycle.* Shambhala.

Asteroids and Chiron

Clow, Barbara Hand. *Chiron: Bridge Between Inner and Outer Planets.* Llewellyn`.

George, Demetra. *Asteroid Goddesses.* Red Wheel/Samuel Weiser.

Michelsen, Neil F., with revisions by Rique Pottenger and text by Zipporah Dobyns. *The Asteroid Ephemeris 1900-2050.* (Ceres, Pallas, Juno, Vesta, Chiron, and the Black Moon Lilith). ACS Publications.

Reinhart, Melanie. *Chiron and the Healing Journey.* Penguin Arkana.

Fixed Stars

Brady, Bernadette. *Brady's Book of Fixed Stars.* Red Wheel/Samuel Weiser.

Ebertin, Reinhold and Georg Hoffmann. *Fixed Stars and Their Interpretation.* AFA.

Robson, Vivian. *Fixed Stars and Constellations in Astrology.* Astrology Classics.

Transits, Progressions, and Directions

Brady, Bernadette. *Predictive Astrology: The Eagle and the Lark.* Red Wheel/Samuel Weiser.

Dobyns, Zipporah. *Progressions, Directions, and Rectification.* TIA Publications.

Forrest, Steven. *The Changing Sky.* ACS Publications.

Hand, Robert. *Planets in Transit.* Whitford Press.

Hastings, Nancy. *Secondary Progressions: Time to Remember.* Red Wheel/Samuel Weiser.

Jayne, Charles. *Progressions and Directions.* Astrological Bureau.

Lundsted, Betty. *Planetary Cycles.* Red Wheel/Samuel Weiser.

Lundsted, Betty. *Transits: The Time of Your Life.* Red Wheel/Samuel Weiser.

March, Marion D. and Joan McEvers. *The Only Way to Learn About Tomorrow.* ACS Publications.

Negus, Joan. *Astro-Alchemy: Making the Most of Your Transits.* ACS Publications.

Negus, Joan. *Astro-Alchemy: Making the Most of Your Transits.* ACS Publications.

Pottenger, Maritha and Zipporah Dobyns, Ph.D. *Unveiling Your Future.* (secondary progressions). ACS Publications.

Robertson, Marc. *The Transits of Saturn.* AFA.

Sakoian, Frances and Louis Acker. *Transits Simplified.* NESA

Sasportas, Howard. *The Gods of Change.* Arkana

Simms, Maria Kay. *Future Signs* (transits, including lunations and eclipses). ACS Publications.

Sullivan, Erin. *Saturn in Transit*. Red Wheel/Weiser

Townley, John. *Astrological Cycles and Life Crisis Periods*. Red Wheel/Samuel Weiser.

Tyl, Noel. *Solar Arcs: Astrology's Most Successful Predictive System*. Llewellyn.

Bibliography, Level III

Dials and Symmetry

Ebertin, Reinhold. *The Combination of Stellar Influences*. AFA

Kimmel, Eleanora. *Cosmobiology for the 21st Century*. AFA.

Harding, Michael and Charles Harvey. *Working with Astrology: The Psychology of Harmonics, Midpoints, and Astro*carto*graphy*. Consider Publications.

Munkasey, Michael. *Midpoints: Unleashing the Power of the Planets*. Book is out-of-print, but is available on CD from www.astrocollege.com.

Simms, Maria Kay. *Dial Detective: Investigation with the 90° Dial, Revised Second Edition*. Cosmic Muse Publications, distributed by Astrolabe, www.alabe.com.

William, Henry. *How to Use Dials*. ACS Publications.

Witte-Lefeldt. *Rules for Planetary Pictures*. Penelope Publications.

Mundane Astrology

Baigent, Michael, Nicholas Campion and Charles Harvey. *Mundane Astrology: An Introduction to the Astrology of Nations and Groups*. Thorson Publishers.

Campion, Nicholas. *The Book of World Horoscopes*. Ordering info at nickcampion.com or BWH@caol.demon.co.uk.

Johndro, L. Edward. *The Earth in the Heavens: Ruling Degrees of Cities and How to Find and Use Them*. Sun Pub. Co.

McEvers, Joan, ed.*The Astrology of the Macrocosm: New Directions in Mundane Astrology*. Llewellyn Publications.

Moore, Moon. *The Book of World Horoscopes*. Seek It Publications (out-of-print, limited availability).

Mundane Astrology: Three Classic Books. Astrology Classics.

> Carter, C.E.O. *An Introduction to Political Astrology*.

> Green, H.S. *Mundane or National Astrology*.

> Raphael's *Mundane Astrology*.

Tyl, Noel. *Prediction in Astrology*. Llewellyn Publications (out-of-print, limited availability).

Horary Astrology

Barclay, Olivia. *Horary Astrology Rediscovered*. Whitford Press.

Cornelius, Geoffrey. *The Moment of Astrology*. Penguin Arkana.

Goldstein-Jacobson, Ivy M. *Simplified Horary Astrology*. AFA.

Hamaker-Zondag, Karen. *Handbook of Horary Astrology*. Red Wheel/Samuel Weiser.

Jones, Marc Edmund. *Horary Astrology*. Aurora Press.

Lavoie, Alphee. *Lose This Book...and

Find It With Horary. A.I.R.

Lilly, William. *Christian Astrology, Book 1 and Book 2*. Ascella Publications

Louis, Anthony. *Horary Astrology, Plain & Simple*. Llewellyn.

March, Marion D. and Joan McEvers. *The Only Way to Learn Horary and Electional Astrology*. ACS Publications.

Scofield, Bruce. *Timing of Events: Electional Astrology*. Astrolabe.

Watters, Barbara. *Horary Astrology and the Judgment of Events*. Valhalla.

Zain, C.C. *Horary Astrology*. Church of Light.

Synastry

Arroyo, Stephen. *Relationships and Life Cycles*. CRCS Publications.

Ashman, Bernie. *Sign Mates: Understanding the Games People Play*. Llewellyn.

Ebertin, Reinhold. *The Cosmic Marriage*. AFA.

Forrest, Steven and Jodie Forrest. *Skymates: Love, Sex and Evolutionary Astrology, Vol. I.*, a new and expanded edition of the synastry classic, Seven Paws Press

Hand, Robert. *Planets in Composite*. Schiffer Publishing.

Lamb, Terry. *Born to Be Together: Astrology, Relationships, and the Soul*. Hay House.

March, Marion D. and Joan McEvers, *The Only Way to Learn About Relationships*. ACS Publications.

Negus, Joan. *Interpreting Composite and Relationship Charts*. ACS Publications.

Neville, E.W. *Planets in Synastry*. Schiffer Publications Ltd.

Pottenger, Maritha. *Starway to Love*. ACS Publications.

Sargent, Lois Haines. *How to Handle Your Human Relations*. AFA.

Townley, John. *Composite Charts: The Astrology of Relationships*. Llewellyn Publications.

Townley, John. *Planets in Love*. Schiffer Publishing.

Solar and Lunar Returns

Merriman, Raymond. *The New Solar Return Book of Prediction*. Seek It Publications.

Shea, Mary. *Planets in Solar Returns: A Yearly Guide for Transformation*. Twin Stars Unlimited.

Volguine, Alexandre. *Technique of Solar Returns*. New York: ASI.

History of Astrology in the West

General

Campion, Nicholas: *The Great Year: Astrology, Millenarianism, and History in the Western Tradition*. *Penguin Arkana*.

Kitson, Annabella, ed. *History and Astrology: Clio and Urania Confer.* Harpercollins

Smoller, Laura Ackerman. *History, Prophecy, and the Stars.* Princeton University Press.

Whitfield, Peter. *Astrology: A History.* British Museum Press and Harry Abrams, Inc.

Mesopotamia and Egypt

Baigent, Michel. *From the Omens of Babylon: Astrology and Ancient Mesopotamia.* Penguin Arkana.

Gleadow, Rupert. *The Origin of the Zodiac.* Jonathan Cape.

Hodson, F.R. *The Place of Astronomy in the Ancient World.* Oxford University Press.

Reiner, Erica and David Edwin Pingree. *Enuma anu Enlil: The Venus Tablets of Ammisaduqua.* Undena Publications.

Krupp. E.C. *In Search of Ancient Astronomies.* McGraw-Hill Book Co.

Lindsay, Jack. *Origins of Astrology.* Barnes & Noble Books.

Neubebauer, O. *Exact Sciences in Antiquity.* Dover Publications.

Thompson, Reginald Campbell. *Reports of the Magicians and Astrologers of Nineveh and Babylon in the British Museum.* Luza and Company/Ams Pr.

Greece and Rome

Barton, Tamsyn. *Ancient Astrology.* Routledge.

Cooper, Jason D. *Mithras: Mysteries and Initiations Rediscovered.* Red Wheel/ Weiser.

Cramer, Frederick. *Astrology in Roman Law and Politics.* Ares Publications.

Cumont, Franz. *Astrology and Religion Among the Greeks and Romans.* Lightning Source, Inc.

Dicks, D.R. *Early Greek Astronomy to Aristotle.* Cornell University Press.

Neugebauer, O. and Henry Bartlett Van Hoesen. *Greek Horoscopes.* American Philosophical Society.

Ptolemy, Claudius. *Tetrabiblos.* Symbols & Signs.

Tester, Jim. *A History of Western Astrology.* Ballantine Books.

Middle Ages

Bonatus, Guido and William Lilly. *Astrologer's Guide.* Lightning Source, Inc.

Kennedy, E.S. and David Pingree. *The Astrological History of Mashaallah.* Harvard University Press.

Parker, Derek. *Familiar to All: William Lilly and Astrology in the Seventeenth Century.* Jonathan Cape.

Thorndike, Lynn. *History of Magic and Experimental Science*, 8 volumes. Lightning Source, Inc.

Wedel, Theodore. *The Medieval Attitude Toward Astrology.* Norwood Editions.

The Renaissance and the Scientific Revolution

Allen, Don Cameron. *The Star-Crossed Renaissance*. Octagon Books (out-of-print, limited availability).

Butterfield, Herbert. *The Origins of Modern Science*. Simon & Schuster.

Caspar, Max, Ed., C. Doris Hellman. *Kepler*. Dover Publications.

Curry, Patrick. *Prophecy and Power: Astrology in Early Modern England*. Polity Press.

French, Peter J. and John Dee. *The World of an Elizabethan Magus*. Routledge and Kegan Paul.

Grafton, Anthony. *Cardano's Cosmos: The Worlds and Works of a Renaissance Astrologer*. Harvard University Press.

Koestler, Arthur. *The Watershed: A Biography of Johannes Kepler*. Rowman & Littlefield Publishers, Inc.

Morin, Jean-Baptiste. *Astrologia Gallica: Book Twenty-Two, Directions*. AFA.

Schumaker, Wayne. *Occult Sciences in the Renaissance*. University of California Press.

Thomas, Keith. *Religion and the Decline of Magic*. Scribner.

Yates, Frances A. *Giordano Bruno and the Hermetic Tradition*. University of Chicago Press.

The Twentieth Century

Howe, Ellic. *Astrology and Psychological Warfare During World War II*. Rider.

History of Astrology

Holden, James Herschel. *A History of Horoscopic Astrology*. AFA.

Naylor, Phyllis Irene Hannah. *Astrology: An Historical Examination*. Maxwell.

Mesopotamian and on-Western Astrology

Mesopotamia

Baigent, Michael. *From the Omens of Babylon: Astrology and Ancient Mesopotamia*. Penguin Arkana.

India

Braha, James T. *Ancient Hindu Astrology for the Modern Western Astrologer*. Hermetician Press.

DeFouw, Hart and Robert Svoboda. *Light on Relationships: The Synastry of Indian Astrology*. Red Wheel/Weiser.

Dreyer, Ronnie Gale. *Vedic Astrology: A Guide to the Fundamentals of Jyotish*. Red Wheel/Samuel Weiser.

Frawley, David. *Astrology of the Seers: A Guide to Vedic/Hindu Astrology*. Morson Pub.

Harness, Dennis, Ph.D. *The Nakshatras: The Lunar Mansions of Vedic Astrology*. Lotus Press.

Roebuck, Valerie J. *The Circle of Stars: An Introduction to Indian Astrology*. Element Books, Ltd.

China

Kermadec, J.M. Huon.de. *The Way to Chinese Astrology*. HarperCollins. (out-of-print, limited availability.

Walters, Derek. *Chinese Astrology: Interpreting the Revelations of the Celestial Messengers*. Natl Book Network.

Mesoamerica

Aveni, Anthony F. *Skywatchers of Ancient Mexico*. University of Texas Press.

Scofield, Bruce. *Day-Signs: Native American Astrology From Ancient Mexico*. One Reed Publications.

Scofield, Bruce. *Signs of Time: An Introduction to Mesoamerican Astrology*. One Reed Publications.

Bibliography, Level IV

Rectification

Simms, Maria Kay, *Dial Detective, Revised 2nd Ed.*, Chpt. 9, "An Introduction to the Use of the Dial for Rectification of Unknown Birth Time," Cosmic Muse Pub., dist. by Astrolabe, www.alabe.com.

Tyl, Noel. *Astrology of the Famed*. Llewellyn.

Tyl, Noel, ed. *Astrology's Special Measurements*, article by Lawrence Ely, "Toward a General Theory of Rectification". Llewellyn Publications.

Tyl, Noel. *Astrology Looks at History*. Llewellyn Publications.

Consulting Track

Anthony, Carol K. Love. *An Inner Connection*. Anthony Publishing Co.

Ashman, Bernie. *Astrological Games People Play*. ACS Publications (out-of-print, available from wwwbernieashman.com).

Bell, Lynn. *Family Threads*. Contact LynnBell@compurserve.com.

Blaschke, Robert. *A Handbook for the Self-Employed Astrologer*. Self-published.

Brennan, Barbara. *Light Emerging*. Bantam New Age.

Brennan, Barbara. *Hands of Light*. Bantam New Age.

Clark, Brian. *The Sibling Constellation*. Penguin Arkana.

Cunningham, Donna. *The Consulting Astrologer's Guidebook*. Red Wheel/Weiser.

Duncan, Adrian. *Astrology: Transformation and Empowerment*. Red Wheel/Samuel Weiser.

Gibson, Mitchell E. *Signs of Mental Illness*. Llewellyn Publications.

Greene, Liz and Howard Sasportas. *The Development of the Personality*. Red Wheel/Samuel Weiser.

Greene, Liz and Howard Sasportas. *The Luminaries: The Psychology of the Sun and Moon in the Horoscope*. Red Wheel/Samuel Weiser.

Greene, Liz and Howard Sasportas. *The Inner Planets: Building Blocks of Personality*. Red Wheel/Samuel Weiser.

Guggenbuhl-Craig, Adolf. *Power in the Helping Professions*. Continuum Intl Pub.

Hamaker-Zondag, Karen. *Psychological Astrology*. Red Wheel/Samuel Weiser.

Hebel, Doris. *Celestial Psychology*. Aurora Press.

Idemon, Richard. *Through the Looking Glass*. Red Wheel/Samuel Weiser.

Kennedy, Eugene and Sara C. Charles, *On Becoming a Counselor: A Basic Guide for Nonprofessional Counselors*. Continuum.

Langs, Robert. *A Clinical Workbook for*

Psychotherapists. Karnac Books.

Lerner, Harriet Goldhor, Ph.D. *The Dance of Anger*. Quill.

Lewis, Byron and Frank Pucelik. *Magic of NLP Demystified*. Metamorphous Press.

McEvers, Joan, ed. *Astrological Counseling: The Path to Self-Actualization*. Llewellyn Publications.

Pottenger, Maritha. *Healing with the Horoscope: A Guide to Counseling*. ACS Publications.

Reid, Linda. *Crossing the Threshold: The Astrology of Dreaming*. Penguin Arkana

Rose, Christina. *Astrological Counseling*. Sterling Pub. Co., Inc.

Tebbs, Carol. *Beyond Basics: Tools for the Consulting Astrologer*, available on CD from www.astrocollege.com or Amazon.com

Tyl, Noel. *Synthesis and Counseling in Astrology*. Llewellyn Publications.

Ethics: Recommended Articles

Arner, David. "ArtPart Forum: Ethics and Confidentiality," *The Mountain Astrologer*, October 1996.

Arner, David. "Ethics in Shades of Grey." *The Mountain Astrologer*, October/November 2001.

Arner, David. "Solving Ethical Problem," *The Astrologers Newsletter*, Boston Chapter NCGR, November 1998.

Arner, David. "Coming to Be...An NCGR Code of Ethics," *NCGR Memberletter*, February/March 1998.

Arner, David. "Ethics Then and Now," *NCGR Memberletter*, November/December 1996.

Betts, Cynthia. "Ethics for the Practice of Astrological Consultation," *NCGR Memberletter*, August/September 1995.

Callahan, Joan, ed. *Ethical Issues in Professional Life*. Oxford University Press. This book contains an especially recommended article "The Ideological Use of Professional Codes" by John Kultgen. The Appendix includes ethics codes for 8 professional organizations.)

Crosby, Beverly. "Wednesday Morning: Reader Response," *NCGR Memberletter*, September 1992.

Cunningham, Donna. "Your Reactions to Clients," *The Mountain Astrologer*, July 1992.

Cunningham, Donna. "First Contact with the Client," *The Mountain Astrologer*, March 1992.

Finger, Lynn. "Astrology and Professionalization: Identifying the Issues," *The Mountain Astrologer*, April/May 1994.

Frigola, Francoise. "Counseling Astrology," *Aspects*, Fall 1990.

Gassman, Paula. "Letters to the Editor," *NCGR Memberletter*, April/May 1997.

Joyce, Linda. "Ethics and Astrology: A Conflict of Interest?" *NCGR*

Memberletter, June/July 1992.

Joyce, Linda. "Setting Boundaries: A Questionnaire," *NCGR Memberletter*, June/July 1992.

Koval, Barbara. "Philosophy and Practice," *The Mountain Astrologer*, August/September 1993.

Lamb, Terry. "Unconscious Communication and the Astrological Consultation," *NCGR Journal*, Winter 2000/2001.

McCabe, Eileen. "Peer Supervision in Astrology," *NCGR Memberletter*, February 1992.

Merriman, Raymond A. "Forecasting Current Events in a Professional Manner," *The Career Astrologer* (PROSIG), January 1995.

Munkasey, Michael. "Towards a Definition of Astrology," *NCGR Memberletter*, February/March 1997.

Oja, Dorothy. "Ethics, Responsibility, and Astrological Conscience," *The Mountain Astrologer*, April/May 1993.

Oja, Dorothy. "More on Ethics and Conscience in Astrology," *The Mountain Astrologer*, November 1994.

Perry, Glenn. "Psychological versus Predictive Astrology," *The Mountain Astrologer*, February/March 1998.

Perry, Glenn. "Toward a Code of Ethics for Astrologers," *The Mountain Astrologer*, October/November 2001.

Potulin, Ruth. "Astrological Standards and Professional Licensing," *The International Astrologer* (International Society for Astrological Research), Summer 2000.

Soffer, Shirley. "The Ten Rules of Right Behavior for Practicing Astrologers," *NCGR Memberletter*, August 1992.

Wright, Jean. "Mindful, Non-Violent Astrology," *The Mountain Astrologer*, March 1993.

Research

Dean, Geoffrey and Arthur Mather. *Recent Advances in Natal Astrology*. The Astrological Association (London).

Foreman, Patricia. *Computers and Astrology*. Good Earth Publications.

Gauquelin, Francoise. *Psychology of the Planets*. ACS.

Gauquelin, Francoise. *Planetary Heredity*. ACS.

Pottenger, Mark. *Astrological Research Methods, Volume I*. ISAR.

Rodden, Lois. *Astro-Data II*. AFA.

Rodden, Lois. *Astro-Data IV*. AFA.

Rodden, Lois. *Astro-Data V*. Data News Press.

Rodden, Lois. *Profiles of Women*. Data News Press.

Sidman, Murray. *Tactics of Scientific Research*. Basic Books.

The NCGR Code of Ehics

Preamble

Astrologers are dedicated to the development and enhancement of the human condition through an understanding of celestial phenomena as applied to human concerns. Astrologers are committed to honesty, fairness and respect for others. Guided by the objective application of astrological technique as well as a commitment to the improvement of the human condition, astrologers seek to increase understanding and compassion

---

**Editors Note About
the Code of Ethics**

NCGR's Constitution and By-Laws, since the first version by the Founders, has held members accountable to a Code of Ethics. The text of this document is available online within www.geocosmic.org accessed from the "About NCGR" title on the banner of home page and then from the banner title "By-laws." See Article XVI–Ethical Principles and Discipline. The current text of the Code of Ethics, published herein, was drafted by David Arner and approved by the Board of Directors in 1968.

---

worldwide. They remain acutely aware of the need to understand themselves in order to understand and help others. Astrologers are aware of the immense contribution astrology can make to human knowledge and wisdom, and accordingly encourage inquiry and an open exchange of ideas both outside and within their profession. And above all, astrologers respect the potential power they hold to affect the lives of others, and accordingly strive for the highest levels of competence and diligence.

A. General Standards

    A.1 Applicability of This Code

    A.2 Avoiding Harm

    A.3 Boundaries of Competence

    A.4 Interpretations and Forecasts

    A.5 Responsibilities to Others

    A.6 Human Differences

    A.7 Personal Problems and Conflicts

    A.8 Sexual Conduct

    A.9 Third Party Services

B. Confidentiality

    B.1 Maintaining Confidentiality

B.2 Consultations with Colleagues

B.3 Confidential Information in Data Collections

C. Advertising and Public Statements

C.1 Definitions

C.2 False and Deceptive Statements

C.3 Unfounded Statements

C.4 Misuse of Astrology

C.5 Organizational Misrepresentation

D. Business Practices

D.1 Solicitation of Clients

D.2 Boundaries

D.3 Referrals

D.4 Fees

D.5 General Practices

E. Teaching and Research

E.1 Accuracy and Objectivity

E.2 Active Participation of Subjects

F. Resolving Ethical Issues

F.1 Confronting Ethical Issues

F.2 Personal and Religious Views

F.3 Cooperating With Ethical Investigations

F.4 Improper Complaints

A. General Standards

A.1 Applicability of This Code

This code applies to the activities of astrologers in their professional work, as well as in their representations and use of astrology at large.

A.2 Avoiding Harm

Astrologers avoid making statements that could cause harm through confusion, misunderstanding or fear.

A.3 Boundaries of Competence

Astrologers provide services to the public- whether in astrology or in other disciplines—only within the boundaries of their competence based on their education, training and appropriate experience.

A.4 Interpretations and Forecasts

a) Consulting astrologers are careful to present their astrological interpretations and opinions with objectivity and appropriate qualifying statements, rather than as final or unequivocal pronouncements.

b) Astrologers make predictions only when they are derived from a conscientious application of technique.

A.5 Responsibilities To Others

a) Astrologers respect the rights of others, including clients, students and colleagues, to hold values, attitudes and opinions different from their own.

b) Astrologers make every effort to refrain from any behavior that may reasonably be considered offensive, harassing or demeaning to others.

c) Consulting astrologers are careful to avoid manipulation of their client's feelings and emotions.

d) Astrologers do not present their interpretations or opinions to their clients in a way that could intimidate them.

A.6 Human Differences

a) Astrologers respect human differences, including those due to astrological configurations, age, gender, race, ethnicity, religion, national origin, disability, sexual gender preference, and socioeconomic status.

b) Should such human differences impair or compromise an astrologer in serving a particular individual or a group, the astrologer makes a conscious effort to ensure fairness and objectivity. Such efforts might include obtaining appropriate training, experience or advice. Otherwise the astrologer should make an appropriate referral.

A.7 Personal Problems and Conflicts

a) Astrologers refrain from counseling individuals or clients with whom they have personal problems or conflicts which may interfere with their effectiveness or cause harm.

b) Astrologers remain alert to personal problems or conflicts arising during an astrology relationship, and take appropriate measures to correct the situation or to limit, suspend or terminate the undertaking.

A.8 Sexual Conduct

a) Astrologers do not engage in sexual behavior with clients or students unless such behavior is clearly separate from and outside of the astrological sessions or work.

b) Astrologers do not engage in sexual harassment. Sexual harassment consists of sexual solicitation, physical advances, or any other verbal or nonverbal sexual conduct that is offensive or that the astrologer should realize might be unwelcome. Sexual harassment can take the form of persistent or pervasive acts, or of a single act that is intense or severe.

A.9 Third -Party Services

a) When an astrologer agrees to provide consulting services for someone at the request of another, the astrologer clarifies the role of the astrologer and the extent of and limits to confidentiality with each party.

b) Astrologers do not attempt to manipulate a person's behavior on behalf of a third party.

B. Confidentiality

B.1 Maintaining Confidentiality

a) Astrologers respect the confidentiality and rights to privacy of their clients, students and others who they deal with in astrological contexts. Confidentiality applies to the identity of and personal information about clients and other individuals.

b) Astrologers do not disclose personal information that is unattainable from public sources without the consent of the person involved as long as that person is living.

B.2 Consultations With Colleagues

When consulting with colleagues, astrologers do not share the identity of the person or persons involved without prior consent. If unavoidable, they share only that information which is necessary to achieve the purposes of the consultation.

B.3 Confidential Information in Data Collections

Astrologers seek permission from living subjects (such as clients, students and friends) before including confidential information in named data collections. Alternatively, astrologers use coding or other techniques to protect the identity of the subjects.

C. Advertising and Public Statements

C.1 Definitions

Advertising, whether paid or unpaid, includes all media, such as magazines, newspaper ads, brochures, business cards, fliers and other printed matter, direct mail promotions, directory listings, resumes, etc. Public statements include advertising as well as statements made in classes, lectures, workshops and other oral presentations, published materials, interviews and comments for use in all electronic media.

C.2 False or Deceptive Statements

a) Astrologers do not make advertising claims or public statements that are false, deceptive, misleading or fraudulent, either because of what they state or suggest, or because of what they omit. This includes claims and statements regarding their training, experience, competence, credentials, organizational affiliations, and services.

b) Astrologers take responsibility for the content of promotional advertising statements made on their behalf.

C.3 Unfounded Statements

Astrologers willingly and openly reveal their sources of information, whether they be scientific, academic, experiential or mystical. Astrologers do not misrepresent their sources of information, and make every effort to verify their accuracy.

C.4 Misuse of Astrology

a) Misuse includes gross misrepresentation of astrological factors used to make sensational and exaggerated claims in public statements.

b) Astrologers are alert to and guard against personal, financial, social, religious, or political factors that might cause them to misuse their influence.

c) Astrologers do not participate in activities in which it appears likely that their expertise or data will be misused by others.

d) If astrologers learn of the misuse of their work, they take reasonable steps to correct or minimize the misuse or misrepresentation.

C.5 Organizational Misrepresentation

a) NCGR members who represent themselves as such are careful to clarify whether they are acting as a spokesperson or as an individual.

b) NCGR members do not act as spokespersons or imply that they are spokespersons for NCGR without the authorization to do so.

D. Business Practices

D.1 Solicitation of Clients

Astrologers do not make astrological statements, predictions or forecasts in the course of the solicitation of clients or students that are misleading either in their optimism or their negativity, or that are frightening or intimidating.

D.2 Boundaries

Astrologers maintain reasonable boundaries with their clients, with the best interests of their clients in mind.

D.3 Referrals

a) Astrologers make referrals based on the best interests of the client or potential client. Astrologers only recommend other professionals who are to the best of their knowledge qualified, competent and ethically responsible.

b) Astrologers do not accept referral fees.

D.4 Fees

Astrologers do not exploit recipients of their services with respect to fees, nor do they misrepresent their fees.

D.5 General Practices

a) Astrologers take responsibility for informing their clients of their business practices, such as length and frequency of sessions and kind of work performed.

b) Astrologers make every effort to honor all commitments they have made.

E. Teaching and Research

E.1 Accuracy and Objectivity

When engaged in teaching or writing, astrologers present astrological information accurately and with appropriate objectivity.

E.2 Active Participation of Subjects

In research projects that involve interviews with research subjects, astrologers are careful to consider the negative impact their questions may have on the well-being of those subjects.

F. Resolving Ethical Issues

F.1 Confronting Ethical Issues

Should an astrologer be uncertain how this Ethics Code may apply in a given situation, the astrologer makes a good faith effort to consult with knowledgeable colleagues, organizational representatives, or with other appropriate authorities in order to choose a proper course of action.

F.2 Personal and Religious Views

a) Astrologers whose personal convictions or religious ethics come into conflict with those of a client or student are alert to the possible compromise of objectivity that may arise. In such cases, astrologers clearly separate their views from their astrological interpretations.

b) Astrologers whose personal convictions or religious ethics come into conflict with this code clarify their differences where appropriate.

F.3 Cooperating With Ethics Investigations

a) Astrologers cooperate in ethics investigations, proceedings and requirements of any organization to which they belong. In doing so, they make reasonable efforts to resolve any issues involving potential breaches of confidentiality.

b) Astrologers are honest in their dealings with ethics bodies. Astrologers do not deceive or withhold appropriate information from ethics bodies.

F.4 Improper Complaints

Astrologers do not file or encourage the filing of ethics complaints that are frivolous and are intended to harm the respondent rather than protect the public.

—Revised October 1998

History of NCGR

At this writing, October 2003, NCGR is in its 32nd year. We've passed our first Saturn Return, a new level of maturity, and with it, a redefining of who we are, as perhaps somewhat differentiated from the intent of our "parents," e.g. the founders of our organization. In seeking to draft a history of NCGR, I at first began with the oral traditions—that which I'd always been told—but then decided to actually consult the oldest archives. That uncovered an interesting dilemma for an astrological organization: there is no absolutely clear record of when the "birth" occurred.

In the one page archive document signed by our first Clerk, Sally Aiken Scanlon, I was able to confirm that March 6, 1971, is indeed a valid birthday for the organization, although obviously there had been previous talks about forming an organization. On that day, a group of seven founders met at 75 Onset Ave., Wareham, Massachusetts, with the intent of taking the official actions that would begin NCGR. The seven incorporators (and intended first Directors) were Harry Darling, M.D., Charles Jayne, Charles Emerson, Sally Aiken Scanlon, Irene Corotneff, Laurel Lowell and Esther Munroe Swift. A notary public, Thomas Castagna, was also present at this meeting. According to Sally Aiken Scanlon, as her signed synopsis appears in our national archive book, the organizational meeting began at 8:40 pm, Dr. Darling presiding. Previously written by-laws were approved, then Charles Jayne was elected Treasurer and Mrs. Scanlon was sworn in as Clerk by Mr. Castagna. The meeting was adjourned at 10:05 pm, and immediately after that, at 10:06 pm, the first "meeting of the Directors of National Council for Geocosmic Research, Inc. was convened, all being present, for the purpose of electing a President. Dr. Darling was unanimously elected by written ballot. The articles of incorporation were signed by all present. The meeting was adjourned by unanimous consent at 10:17 pm." NCGR's stamped certificate of incorporation under the laws of the State of Massachusetts is dated a few days later, on March 11, 1971.

Now comes a curious and interesting question for an astrological organization: what time was the official begin-

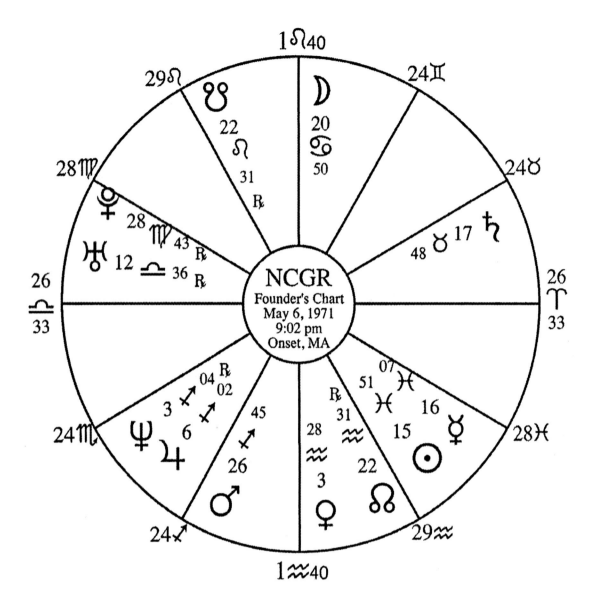

ning? In the archives, right after the Scanlon summary of this first meeting, is a chart for NCGR that was calculated by Neil F. Michelsen's Astro Computing Services in 1976. The chart is set for 9:02 pm, a time that is not mentioned anywhere within Mrs. Scanlon's documentation, or anywhere else among archive documents. Obviously this cannot be the moment of signing the articles of incorporation, because according to the minutes, this did not occur until sometime between 10:06 and 10:17. The 9:02 chart has long been considered to be THE chart, and the fact that it is two minutes past 9:00 pm rather than on the hour certainly suggests that it is an election chart. Apparently this chart is an oral tradition passed down by founders who, unfortunately, are no longer here to query as to why, or why they failed to clearly record it! The chart seems to work, so we'll let it stand, though it would be nice to know upon what it is based. One reasonably logical guess: it was the time of the official swearing in

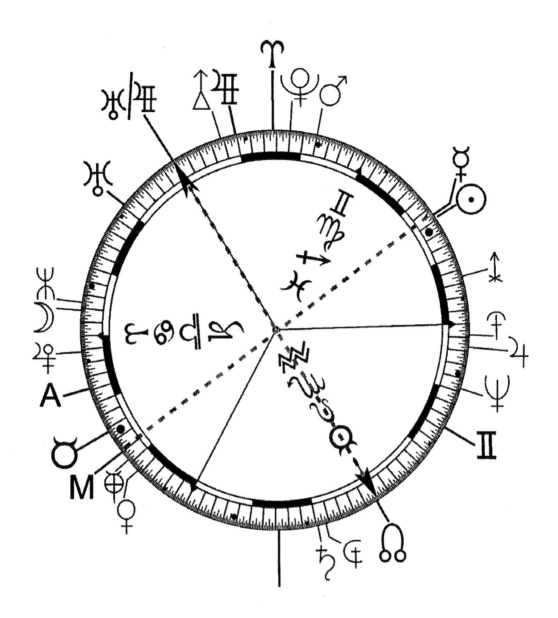

Founders Chart for NCGR shown in Dial Format

by the notary of Mrs. Scanlon, who as Clerk, was also the first official Massachusetts agent, a post required by law for a Massachusetts incorporation. Why Mrs. Scanlon did not record that time is anyone's guess!

An additional note on the Founder's Chart: although we currently tend to use as our chart the standard wheel that appears on our website, with conventional Ascendant based on Koch (or Placidus)

Houses, the chart in the archive book is in the Meridian House system. This is indicative of the Hamburg School, Uranian Astrology, that is known to have been the focus of at least some, if not all, of the founders. Though NCGR's educational perspective currently covers a broad perspective of astrological technique, emphasizing the Hamburg School no more than a variety of other specialties, a bit of Uranian astrological speculation on why the founders (probably) chose 9:02 pm is of historical interest (as well as admittedly a special interest of mine, as well). The illustrations show both the standard chart (with Koch houses), and a 90° dial chart (a primary tool of the Uranian and Cosmobiology systems). The dial chart shows one astrological reason why the 9:02 pm time may have been elected. The fast-moving Midheaven degree at that time is key to a planetary picture that a group of founders interested in Uranian Astrology would have wanted to be prominent in their inception chart.

From other letters in the archives describing the early years of the organization, the Meridian Ascendant in Scorpio has its descriptive merits. Ruled by Mars or Pluto (take your pick), in square with each other in the Founder's Chart, squabbles emerged almost immediately among these academics over just about everything from how meetings should be conducted to dissatisfaction over whether something should be done to come up with a better birth time! In November of 1971, 20 members were listed, of which 8 were considered "charter." The eight included Ruth Oliver, Thomas Glynn and Edgar Wagner. First, Charles Jayne and, later, Dr. Darling had resigned over various disagreements. Despite rocky beginnings, somehow the organization grew, and has continued to grow slowly but surely over the years. I have no idea when the shift occurred after which it became common practice to illustrate the organization's chart with standard chart wheel (Koch or Placidus houses) with Libra rising, but it appears to have reflected an increasing note of harmony and balance that surely con-

tributed to a growth in membership as the 70s decade progressed into the 80s.

A May 1973 list in the archives has 72 members, and Director's names, including several who are very familiar to today's astrologers: Eleanor Bach, Secretary; Zipporah Dobyns, Ph.D., Director; Professor Kenneth Negus, Editor; Rob Hand, Research Coordinator and Frances Sakoian, Public Relations Director. By this time, the focus of NCGR had already begun to evolve at least somewhat differently from its beginnings. The organization began with a highly academic focus on serious scientific research correlating astrology to other fields, such as medicine. Now the primary thrust shifted to a broader format of education and publishing geared toward raising the standards and status of astrologers.

By 1976 NCGR had been granted non-profit status (federal 501(c) 3), was publishing a newsletter and a journal, and was regularly holding conferences. About a dozen local chapters had been formed as the decade drew to a close. A prime mover in the first decade of NCGR was a man who never served as its Chairman, Charles Emerson of New York City. Charles served sometimes as treasurer, sometimes as secretary, and sometimes both, but always as the one who kept things going, recruited and mentored others, and who served NCGR with absolute dedication and seemingly endless energy. For this reason, he has often and most deservedly been called "the Father of NCGR."

NCGR's first three heads, which sometime shortly after that first meeting came to be identified as Chairman rather than President, were medical doctors. Succeeding Dr. Darling were Henry Altenberg, M.D., and then Donald Wharton, M.D., who served until 1981, when a businessman and computer programmer, Neil F. Michelsen, who was founder of Astro Computing Services and programmer of *The American Ephemeris*, became Chairman. Neil continued in leadership of NCGR until his death in May of 1990, after which Rob Hand became Chairman. I was privileged to become the first woman elected to head NCGR, after Rob retired at the end of 1998. Because some board members objected to the term Chairwoman and others (including myself) disliked the politically correct "Chairperson," the term Chairman was officially shortened to Chair.

The 1980s saw a strong surge in NCGR's growth, lead by an active and dedicated board of Directors, most of whom were now active, practicing professional astrologers. Among them, a prime mover was Mary Downing, who served as Executive Secretary throughout the decade and into the 90s. If Charles is called "the Father of NCGR," Mary could rightfully be called "the Mother." Although Mary was more years than not in the background, as Production Designer or mentor for others in regard to our NCGR Publications, it is much to her credit that they became of such high quality. Mary recruited and mentored me, after I was first elected to the board in 1982, and together we revived the *NCGR Journal*, that had faltered and not been published for several years prior. The "Phoenix" issue was published in the summer of 1984, becoming the first of many magazines of professional quality in both con-

tent and appearance. Mary also promoted the establishment of *Memberletter*. Through the years she continued to be a major contributor to the design and quality of our publications, though she also worked tirelessly to promote NCGR in every way, including the recruitment and mentoring of others who became NCGR leaders. Notable among these is Madalyn Hillis-Dineen who was for several years Memberletter Editor, then Executive Secretary and has been for several recent years, our Clerk (NCGR lingo for corporate secretary). Many successful conferences were held during Mary's "heyday" as Executive Secretary, in quite a number of cities, as she actively worked with other board members and host local chapters.

A very major achievement of the 1980s and onward to the present is NCGR's Education and Certification Program, devised by a group of skilled, dedicated people who originated and led its pre-planning, launch and implementation. Beginning with an initial curriculum by Education Director Professor Kenneth Negus, Ph.D. in the late 70s, a wide-scale program involving all of NCGR's chapters was launched at Princeton University in 1979. Key people in the organization of the Princeton seminar were Ken and his successor as Education Director, Sonny Delmonico, with Joan Negus, Joanna Shannon and Lenore Canter. Following the opening meetings, an Education Committee came into being under the leadership of Joan and Joanna, who became Co-Directors of Education. A new curriculum, testing and certification program was gradually developed and implemented which has become the hallmark of NCGR, internationally respected for its excellence. A more detailed profile of the NCGR Education and Certification Program appears in the Forward to this publication.

NCGR in 2003

Currently NCGR has about 2400 members, most of whom are affiliated with one of our chapters. Chapters are local subsidiary organizations having a minimum of ten NCGR members in good standing who have agreed to an organizational structure compatible with NCGR's Constitution and By-Laws. As of this writing, there are 40 chapters and a few more in process of forming. Chapters are legal extensions of NCGR national, and thus have certain financial and organizational reporting requirements. One-third of annual national dues for every chapter-affiliated member are rebated to his or her chapter as a contribution to the chapter's operating funds.

NCGR also sponsors Special Interest Groups (SIGs) that are not bound by geographical location, but share their interest and study in a specific astrological discipline through newsletters and online. It is also possible for a local or regional astrological organization that does not wish to become a chapter to instead become an Affiliate of NCGR. Affiliates have no reporting requirements, nor do they receive member rebates, but they do have a link with NCGR that provides for announcements of events and networking.

A Board of Directors that includes three elected officers administers the organization as a whole. Officers are the Chair, the Clerk (secretary of the corporation) and the Treasurer. There are five elected Directors. All elected board members serve for three year terms. One officer is up for election each year, and two (or one) of the Directors, so that there will always be some returning members for continuity. The position of Chair is limited to two terms. Each year after election results are in, the Elected Board meets to discuss which departmental functions its members are best qualified and willing to handle, and then they appoint (by recommendation of the Chair) Directors for five additional positions to serve for one-year terms. The Appointed Directors are specifically chosen for their expertise and ability to manage important NCGR departments. Because our Education Department has such a key role in NCGR and a large amount of work to manage, two Co-Directors are appointed to head it. Board members serve as volunteers, but we also have some staff personnel who are compensated. The chief of staff is our Executive Director. Staff positions include Memberletter Editor and Webmaster, and we also employ by a bid process professional graphics assistance for various publishing projects.

Many of NCGR's local chapters sponsor speakers and/or classes, and the national organization sponsors occasional larger conferences, such as the 2001 Education Conference in Hartford, Connecticut and the 2003 Education Conference in Minneapolis, MN. Plans are under discussion to reestablish a series of Master Classes, similar to those that were popular NCGR gatherings in the 1980s.

Six informative Memberletters containing organizational news and timely articles on astrology are published annually. Our magazine, *Geocosmic Journal*, is published twice annually. It has a featured theme with a guest editor and several articles by specialists in the theme, plus a variety of other articles. In 2003, the first GJs published featured Mundane Astrology and Peace, guest edited by Stephanie Clement, and the second featured Business and Financial Astrology, guest edited by Grace Morris. Other periodically updated publications include Memberlist and a Directory of Professional Astrologers.

This publication, the 2003 edition of NCGR Education Curriculum and Study Guide for Certification Testing is the first of what is projected to be an increasing number of print-on-demand publications to be made available through our Executive Director's office or our website http://www.geocosmic.org. New technology has made it possible to produce short runs of perfect bound books with color covers without a substantial upfront investment, so we intend to make available a series of these. Next on the schedule for this project will be anthologies of research papers submitted for Level IV certification.

NCGR has a tiered membership program that encourages an easy method for members to make tax deductible donations over and above their annual membership dues for the support of their choice of NCGR's special funds: Lucy Titunik Health and Welfare Fund, the Building Fund, the Neil F. Michesen Headquarters Fund and the General Fund.

For further detailed information about NCGR's current activities and offerings we invite you to surf our web site, www.geocosmic.org. It features a growing number of articles of interest from back issues of our magazine, listings and links to our various chapters and SIGS, plus a sophisticated search engine to help you contact our Level IV certified astrologers, each of whom is entitled to a page with photo, biography and a listing of services. On our site you'll learn of events, find free features, be able to participate in research projects through our research page, learn where you can find teachers either in local areas or through online services, easily access our a secure shopping area through which you can join, renew membership, register for conferences or purchase publications and conference tapes. You'll discover chat lists you can join, and much more...with more to come.

NCGR's motto is "Building Community through Astrological Research and Education." We welcome you as an active participant in our community!

—*Maria Kay Simms, Chair*

Program for Applying Schools Equivalency Criteria

An applying school's curriculum would need to meet the criteria of NCGR's Study Guide. An applying school may meet only Level I, or Levels I and II, or they may meet Levels I, II and III. In the case of the latter, an applicant would only need to apply for Level IV, and subsequently, professional certification. There would be no equivalency program for any school that would encompass Level IV certification, no matter if the school's curriculum included the material required for Level IV certification. Level IV would must be taken to its completion by each applicant in their desired track of certification.

A school applying for Equivalency, must submit a school purpose, description of the curriculum and the syllabus for each course taught. The grading system must be explained and how the classes are conducted.

An applying school's curriculum must follow NCGR's guidelines. Using the Study Guide, its curriculum must include the following:

Level I

The curriculum must provide the building blocks in the foundation of Western astrology. The curriculum must provide a comprehensive education in the signs, planets, houses, personal points (Ascendant, Midheaven and Moon's Nodes); hemisphere emphasis and quadrants; major aspects and major configurations; and finally, the delineation of the topics listed. An introduction in basic astronomical phenomena is necessary, such as retrogradation, eclipses and solstices. As well, the curriculum must be structured to provide proficiency in natal chart and planetary calculations for the northern and southern hemispheres, and east and west of Greenwich. Elementary material in Ancient and Medieval astrology must be introduced.

Level II

As well as the continuation and comprehensiveness of the criteria for Level I[1], the following must be added to the delineations:

a. minor aspects
b. lunar phases
c. derived houses
d. fixed stars

Calculations include:

a. progressions (and their interpretation)

b. solar arc directions (and their interpretation)

c. the application of transits (and their interpretation)

d. Vertex (and its interpretation)

e. the Equatorial Ascendant (and its interpretation)

f. antiscia (solstice points) (and their interpretation)

Mundane charting, such as ingress charts is required. Ancient and medieval astrology must have stronger coverage, as well as some other astrological disciplines, such as Vedic (Hindu) astrology

Level III

For a school to meet the equivalency for Level III, the curriculum must thoroughly cover all the information included in Levels I and II. The curriculum must cover:

a. the use the 360° and 90° dials precisely

b. horary and electional astrology

c. Synastry

d. solar and lunar returns
e. History
f. Vedic, Mesoamerican and Chinese astrology must be surveyed
g. Ancient/Medieval astrology

An applying school for any Level of certification must meet the following criteria:

The school's instructor(s) must have hands-on relationships with the student. This may be in a physical or private, on-line classroom; via e-mail or telephone; or written correspondence.

There must be written homework, which include essays, delineations and calculations.

There must be exams that reflect the student's ability to recall subject matter.

There must be grades that reflect the student's attendance or participation, homework, and exams.

A graduate[2] from an applying school may apply to NCGR's Education Board of Examiners[3] for approval, at which time the applicant may take the next exam he or she is authorized to take. The school must provide the applicant's transcript at the time of his or her application.

Notes

Notes

Notes

Notes